"*Accessing the Riches of Heaven* is packed with insight into the ways of abundance and connects us to the greater purpose of the riches that God has made available to us. The declarations at the end of each chapter are phenomenal and will now be a core part of my prayer life."

Jamie Galloway, Jamie Galloway Ministries; prophetic communicator; author, *Secrets of the Seer*

"It is God's passion for us to live an abundant life. This is what Jesus said in John 10:10. My friend Patricia King does an outstanding job in revealing some critical secrets to living this life on many levels. I truly believe as you read *Accessing the Riches of Heaven*, you will discover meaningful truths to unlock this level of living."

Robert Henderson, global apostolic leader; author, *Operating in the Courts of Heaven*; Robert Henderson Ministries

"Everywhere I travel I meet people needing guidance about finances. Patricia King's new book, *Accessing the Riches of Heaven*, provides a new and divinely inspired set of guidelines for believers who want to live in God's abundance rather than from paycheck to paycheck. Read it and live on a higher plane now."

Joan Hunter, healing evangelist; author

"Patricia King leads us on a journey into the supernatural realms of heavenly provision and opens up a treasure chest of abundance. We're given not only an impartation of faith to see it, but also the courage to reach in and receive it. There is unlimited supply available in the glory. You will be blessed as you read!"

Joshua Mills, International Glory Ministries

"Heaven contains immeasurable riches—revelation, wisdom, gifts, miracles, wealth and wonder. Patricia King will take you there on a journey of *Accessing the Riches of Heaven*. This book is a map, a light to lead you into God's true calling for your life. You need to read this book!"

Brian Simmons, The Passion Translation Project; Passion & Fire Ministries

"Patricia has really done it! Filled with fantastic teaching and practical instruction, *Accessing the Riches of Heaven* will help readers access the abundant life and unlock the riches of heaven by tapping into the truth of God's Word. It is a life changer!"

Ward Simpson, president and CEO, GOD TV

"*Accessing the Riches of Heaven* is the best book I have read on living in the abundant life of Christ. My faith soared as I read it. God not only wants to make you wealthy, but wants to give you access to all the riches and glory of heaven! As you read you will be amazed at God's heart of abundance toward you."

Matt Sorger, prophetic minister; author, Power for Life; television host; Matt Sorger Ministries

"*Accessing the Riches of Heaven* is a practical guide, challenging us to appropriate all that Jesus has provided for us. As revelation opens our eyes to Kingdom realities, faith, born of the Spirit, arises in our hearts and we become world transformers. This book will assist you in taking each of these steps."

Dr. Mark Virkler, president, Christian Leadership University

"God is our never-ending source of life and abundance. Do you believe that for your own life? Patricia King's book, *Accessing the Riches of Heaven*, will cause you to dream much bigger with God and really believe that the treasury room of heaven is open for you. This book with push you to the next level of faith."

Ana Werner, seer; international speaker; author, *The Seer's Path* and *Seeing behind the Veil*

"Patricia King hits it out of the park when it comes to accessing the riches of heaven and light invading darkness. She's called to invade darkness by releasing heaven on earth. This book is Patricia King. She models in an amazing way what she is writing about. This book will help you access heaven and then release God's glorious riches in the midst of darkness."

Barbara J. Yoder, lead apostle, Shekinah Regional Apostolic Center; Breakthrough Apostolic Ministries Network

ACCESSING THE RICHES OF HEAVEN

ACCESSING THE RICHES OF HEAVEN

KEYS TO EXPERIENCING GOD'S LAVISH PROVISION

PATRICIA KING

a division of Baker Publishing Group
Minneapolis, Minnesota

Published by Chosen Books
11400 Hampshire Avenue South
Bloomington, Minnesota 55438
www.chosenbooks.com

Chosen Books is a division of
Baker Publishing Group, Grand Rapids, Michigan

Printed in the United States of America

ISBN 978-0-8007-9937-3

Library of Congress Cataloging-in-Publication Control Number: 2018053593

Cover design by Rob Williams, InsideOutCreativeArts

19 20 21 22 23 24 25 7 6 5 4 3 2 1

In keeping with biblical principles of creation stewardship, Baker Publishing Group advocates the responsible use of our natural resources. As a member of the Green Press Initiative, our company uses recycled paper when possible. The text paper of this book is composed in part of post-consumer waste.

Contents

Foreword

I just read *Accessing the Riches of Heaven* and went on a true learner's journey. I feel as if I had an experience and deepening of some core truths that have expanded in me. And you will, too!

Growing up as a second-generation Christian, I noticed a stark difference between my parents and me. They had escaped hard lives and some really difficult family dynamics and came into an amazing church experience that redefined their identities. They were excited about one day going to heaven and, like most Christians in the 1980s, loved the concept of bringing people to salvation so that they, too, could enjoy eternal life in heaven.

One of my deepest character flaws, I realized as I was growing up, is impatience. I get crowd anxiety in Disney because I just want to be on the ride. When planes are landing, I get frustrated waiting as we circle the airport trying to find the perfect landing conditions. When I am hungry, I want to eat instantly. With my faith, I realized I was frustrated because

I had been taught all my life that the Kingdom of heaven does break in, but only as a taste or glimpse of what is to come. That discouraged me, and I had only two options in my young faith: (1) to go to heaven faster or (2) to find an alternative truth.

So began my quest for trying to find out what fullness of faith looks like in my life. I studied and meditated on what the prayer of John 17 really means when Jesus asked the Father to let us be one as they are one, and to see His glory. He was praying for access for all believers to the Father's original intention and for the power through the Holy Spirit to manifest His original plan. I realized—through an albeit aggressive pursuit—that I could never be satisfied with one day going to heaven as my primary divine motivator. I became obsessed with seeing the riches of heaven manifested on the earth, on this side of eternity, the way Jesus modeled it.

When you see the Bible this way—that God has given you the gift of time on earth but that He wants to fill your time with His beautiful nature and original plan for you while you become a catalyst for breakthrough for others through your own faith—it changes the way you live. It changes the way you pray. And it especially changes your expectations in life.

Because of the glimpses I have seen of the Kingdom of heaven manifesting, I am living a radically different life than if I were made by my own desires, skills and talents, navigating even the Bible with my own understanding. Accessing heaven has led me personally into experiencing the power of His healing in my life and body. It has led me to discover the destiny and purpose He has revealed to me. And accessing heaven has allowed me to walk in justice over major social issues. He has given birth to compassion in me. I have had supernatural encounters that have created a different life from what I could scarcely have hoped for or dreamed of (see Ephesians 3:20).

So I am grateful for Patricia's book. It is honest and vulnerable. You will find spiritual intelligence inside these pages for some of the hunger pains you have felt for a very long time. She brings out beautifully a model of what accessing the riches of heaven looks like for a believer's life now. The biblical truth through the filter of Patricia's experience with God and with life will mentor you and give you a huge new divine motivator (or reinforce the one you already have)—that God wants to be with you where you are now and give you access to what He always intended for you and the world around you through you.

This book will also act as a reset in some areas that may have blocked you from seeing what holds heaven back in your life. Patricia is a teacher, and you are going on a well-constructed, step-by-step process to rebuild your faith to access heaven and gain the perspective that you really are seated in heavenly places. She takes charismatic words that have been buzzwords—sometimes scary or marginalizing words—and places them back within their context, so that when you hear words like *ascending* or *portals*, it is not just poetry or fringy experiential slang but part of your biblical truth of ways that God can give you access.

We have so much more to live for if only we can gain perspective for what is available through Christ. This book will take you on a heart and faith journey to access what is already yours. Ultimately, we are called to fill this earth with the riches of heaven, and I want to encourage you to answer the questions Patricia includes here very personally, and make the declarations she gives you, as you allow God to transform your perspective and give you one of Jesus' main divine motivators He promised you: that His Kingdom will come in your life on earth as it is in heaven.

Shawn Bolz, host, *Exploring the Prophetic* podcast; author, *Translating God*, *God Secrets*, *Modern Prophets* and *Growing Up with God*; bolzministries.com

1

On Earth as It Is in Heaven

> Your kingdom come. Your will be done, on earth as it is in heaven.
>
> Matthew 6:10

"I just want to get out of here!"

I was caught off guard by this blunt expression of anguish from a middle-aged Christian woman whom I knew fairly well. We were enjoying an amiable visit together during a walk on a beautiful sunny day, so I was shocked when these dark and despairing words were injected into our conversation.

"Out of where?" I asked. I stopped walking and turned toward her in order to hear her explanation. "Do you want to move out of this area?"

Her eyes dropped from my gaze and fell into a solemn and depressed stare toward the ground. After a few seconds of silence she whispered, "No, I mean out of 'here.' . . . I want to go to heaven."

I had no idea she had been struggling, as she appeared outwardly to be quite happy and content. What had prompted this sudden desire to exit the earth?

"Living here is just so hard," she confided. "I am dealing with health issues, financial restraints and some domestic hardships, and I am just tired. I want out. I want to go to heaven."

She is not the only one who has ever felt that way. Perhaps you are thinking, *Hmmm, I have had some of those thoughts myself at times.* Having such ponderings does not mean you are suicidal. My friend was not suicidal either. She just wanted to escape the pressures and trials of living in this world. In fact, I have had such thoughts myself. I remember thinking years ago, when I was going through some intense pressures, *I just want to be in heaven.* I was neither suicidal nor depressed; I simply wanted to enter a place of peace that I could not seem to find.

Every human has innate knowledge that he or she was created for a heavenly and divine state—a realm of peace, tranquility, pleasure and abundance where everything is reconciled into God's goodness and righteousness. In heaven there is no injustice, no sin, sickness, sorrow, death, oppression, depression, lack or poverty. The atmosphere of heaven is one of ecstasy, peace, worship and extravagance. God's victorious "love presence" fills every moment and every place in heaven with eternal bliss.

The Devastating Event

You and I were created for this glorious state of existence. It has been God's intention from the beginning of time. We read in the first chapter of Genesis that when God created the earth and everything in it, it was all good—very good! There was no sin, sickness, disease, oppression or poverty. To Adam and Eve, those were all foreign and unknown. They lived in a heavenly atmosphere with God at their side, spending time together in unbroken fellowship. In the days prior to their fatal fall, it was indeed "on earth as it is in heaven."

Then a cataclysmic event took place in the Garden: Humans sinned. As a result, all the consequences of sin flooded into the earth and were infused into the very nature of man. Romans 6:16 explains:

> Do you not know that when you present yourselves to someone as slaves for obedience, you are slaves of the one whom you obey, either of sin resulting in death, or of obedience resulting in righteousness?

Adam and Eve disobeyed God willfully and submitted to the devil, becoming his slaves. God had entrusted them with the authority to rule the earth, but at that moment the earth became the devil's domain. Satan became the "god of this world" and exercised his legal right to usher his evil kingdom into the earth—complete with all its darkness, pain and oppression. As centuries went by and the population of the earth increased, the weight of oppression intensified because the masses yielded to the devil's temptations and deceptions. Instead of the earth bearing fruit unhindered, it bore thistles. Instead of peace in the atmosphere, there was unrest. Instead of people receiving abundance without effort, they now had to labor with intensity to overcome lack.

You and I understand only too well the pain and discomfort of this fallen state. At times, all of us have expected fruitfulness and abundance, only to discover that unfulfilled dreams and expectations were our portion. This type of outcome will always leave us discouraged because life was never intended to be that way.

What if I told you that you can live on earth in a realm of riches and abundance in all things? Would you think this possible? Would you want to lay hold of that promise?

God's Original Intent

God's original intent was to create humankind in His image and likeness and to set this pinnacle of creation on the earth as His children to enjoy unbroken fellowship with Him and with one another. He wanted them to be encompassed by and saturated with His glory, to exercise dominion and to experience the abundance of every good and glorious thing in life—"on earth as it is in heaven."

Even though we sinned and erected a barrier of separation that seemingly sabotaged His original intent, He had already planned from before the foundation of the world to overcome it all and to restore us as His children.

What was His plan? To become a man and pay the full price of redemption for our sin. In other words, His solution was to buy us back with His own life. In order to accomplish His goal, the Son of God laid aside His prerogatives as God (see Philippians 2:6–8[1]) and became man. As a man He would need to fulfill all the Law and the prophets, living without sin in thought, word and deed. One slip would destroy everything. If He yielded to just one temptation, then even as the first man, Adam, became ruled by the devil, so also would Jesus. This was a tightrope to walk on. His love for us and His desire for us to live in His heavenly realm were greater than the risk He was compelled to take. His motivation? His great love and unquenchable desire for us.

Jesus was undeterred by the impossible task before Him. We can see a picture of His determination in the life of David. While he was on the run from King Saul, David and his men were living in a town named Ziklag, in Philistine territory. When they returned from battle one day, they found the town burned to the ground and their women and children taken into captivity. "David and his men wept aloud until they had no strength left to weep" (1 Samuel 30:4 NIV). David's men were so bitter that they talked about stoning him (see verse 6).

Then the Bible offers us two keys. First, "David found strength in the LORD his God" (verse 6). And second, David got the go-ahead from the Lord to pursue, overtake and recover from the enemy their women, children and all their possessions. He and his men were successful: "Nothing was missing: young or old, boy or girl, plunder or anything else they had taken. David brought everything back" (verse 19).

Like David at Ziklag, Jesus' goal was to pursue, overtake and recover everything plundered by the enemy. Jesus was empowered by the Holy Spirit at His baptism when the Holy Spirit came upon Him, and He set out with unconditional, passionate love to redeem the human race from their sin.

You, too, may have or currently are experiencing loss and devastation in your life. Even though you have been saved by the blood of Jesus and by His death and resurrection on your behalf, you may, like David, have experienced loss and wept until you had no more tears to weep. I encourage you, like David, to find strength in the Lord, and then to pursue, overtake and recover everything that has been lost. We will explore in the rest of this book just how to do this, and how it is that you can access the riches of heaven, bringing them into manifestation in your life here on earth.

Two Kingdoms Reign

A kingdom is the domain and jurisdiction of a king's rule. A kingdom is not a democracy because the king is sovereign. The majority does not rule; the king does.

We find in Christ's teaching that there are two conflicting kingdoms in the realm of the spirit. For instance, when the Pharisees accused Jesus of casting out demons by the power of Beelzebul, the ruler of demons, He explained:

> Any kingdom divided against itself is laid waste. . . . If Satan also is divided against himself, how will his kingdom stand? For you say that I cast out demons by Beelzebul. . . . But if I cast out demons by the finger of God, then the kingdom of God has come upon you."
>
> Luke 11:17–18, 20

Jesus made clear His intention to conquer the devil's kingdom and to establish God's Kingdom.

The following chart offers you an overview of the two kingdoms:

	Kingdom of God	Kingdom of Satan
Rulers	Jesus is King (1 Timothy 1:17)	Satan is king (Luke 11:18)
Spiritual entities	Angels sent by God (Hebrews 1:14)	Rulers, authorities, powers of this dark world and spiritual forces of evil in heavenly realms (Ephesians 6:12)
Citizens	The redeemed (Colossians 1:13)	The lost (Colossians 1:13)
Atmosphere	Light, love, peace, righteousness, bliss, goodness, blessing (Galatians 5:22–23)	Darkness, hate, fear, evil, terror, malevolence (Galatians 5:19–21)
King's word that prevails in the kingdom	Truth (John 14:6)	Deception, error, lies (John 8:44)
Law that governs	The law of the spirit of life in Christ Jesus (Romans 8:2)	The law of sin and death (Romans 8:2)
Economy	Abundant and stable, based on faith, generosity and God's provisional promises (John 10:10; 2 Peter 1:3–4)	Unstable, based on worldly currencies, selfishness and greed (Revelation 18)
Eternal state	In glory for all eternity: rewards (2 Timothy 2:10)	In torment for all eternity: hell, fire, brimstone (Revelation 20:10)

Both kingdoms are very real, and we choose which kingdom we will live in by choosing which king we serve. Clearly it is wisest to choose Him, the King of all kings. Jesus came to take us out of the kingdom of darkness and to translate us into the Kingdom of light. His Kingdom is not something that will come in the future. His Kingdom is *now.* When a person comes to Christ, he or she enters the Kingdom.

The Kingdom of Heaven Is at Hand

As I mentioned earlier, when Jesus came to the earth He had to fulfill all righteousness as a man (even though He was God) in order to purchase us back from our sinful state:

> Although He existed in the form of God, [He] did not regard equality with God a thing to be grasped, but emptied Himself, taking the form of a bond-servant, and being made in the likeness of men. Being found in appearance as a man, He humbled Himself by becoming obedient to the point of death, even death on a cross.
>
> Philippians 2:6–8

Christ began His ministry by submitting to the waters of baptism. John did not understand at first, even though he recognized that Jesus was the Lamb of God—the Messiah. But it was necessary because the waters of baptism represent repentance from sin, and although Jesus did not need to repent because He had never sinned, He knew that unless all righteousness could be fulfilled, no mere human could be made right with God. We could not do it on our own, so in the waters of baptism Jesus repented on our behalf.

In other words, you have the ability to repent because He already repented "as you." You have grace to enter repentance due to Christ's actions on your behalf in the waters of baptism. Everything Jesus engaged in to fulfill righteousness was "as you." We cannot take credit for anything. Worthy is the Lamb! Oh, how this stirs deep worship in us when we realize that we cannot even repent without His grace!

After Jesus' baptism, the heavens were open over Him: "Behold, the heavens were opened, and he saw the Spirit of God descending as a dove and lighting on Him" (Matthew 3:16). We read in Deuteronomy 28:23 that due to our sin and disobedience the heavens are like brass. Through repentance, however, the heavens are opened. Through Christ's act of obedience in baptism, the heavens were opened over him, and they still are. If Jesus lives in you, then the heavens are opened over your life, too, and you have access into that heavenly realm of blessing through your faith.

Following His baptism, Jesus was led into the wilderness to endure the devil's temptation on our behalf. Through this experience and throughout His life He was tempted "in all things as we are, yet without sin" (Hebrews 4:15). Like Christ, you have power to resist temptation also, because He did it for you and *as* you.

Following His wilderness experience, He settled in Capernaum and preached repentance, saying that the Kingdom of heaven "is at hand" (Matthew 4:17). That was His message. He did not preach church growth; He preached the Kingdom of heaven (although authentic, God-initiated church growth will most likely follow powerful preaching about the Kingdom of heaven!).

Through the fall of humankind, sin "brassed over" the heavens to prohibit people from entering into the Kingdom of heaven, but in Christ, we now have access to the Kingdom of heaven with all its riches! He repented "as us" and resisted sin as us in order to grant us this very access. When you are one with Christ, living the life He graciously gave you through His finished work on the cross, sin is no longer blocking your way, brassing over your access to heaven.

Kingdom Power on Earth

Jesus not only preached, "Repent for the Kingdom of heaven is at hand," He modeled the Kingdom of heaven. Where there was sickness, He healed. Where there was demonization, He cast out devils. Where there was death, He resurrected. Where there was defilement, He cleansed. And where there was hunger, He filled and satisfied. He brought the atmosphere of heaven to earth. He ushered in the Kingdom of heaven everywhere He went.

Look at this account of Christ's ministry:

> And Jesus went about all Galilee, teaching in their synagogues, preaching the gospel of the kingdom, and healing all kinds of sickness and all kinds of disease among the people. Then His fame went throughout all Syria; and they brought to Him all sick people who were afflicted with various diseases and torments, and those who were demon-possessed, epileptics, and paralytics; and He healed them. Great multitudes followed Him.
>
> Matthew 4:23–25 NKJV

Wherever the Kingdom of heaven is made manifest, crowds will gather. That is why even to this day crowds gather around authentic heavenly manifestations of miracles, signs and wonders. We are drawn to this heavenly dimension. We were created for this glory. We were not created for sickness and oppression. We were created for the realm of heaven—the realm of God. This realm is full of His riches—riches of peace, health, wholeness, provision, safety and freedom.

Jesus' very purpose was to destroy the works of the devil, to remove his power over the earth and break his rulership over man (see 1 John 3:8[2]) in order for us to receive the fullness of His riches in heaven.

The Dream of God

Bill Johnson preaches, "The dream of God is to be discovered and embraced until it becomes our dream."[3] God's dream is that the Kingdom of heaven will come to earth and that we, His children, will experience all the blessings of His riches in heaven. When it becomes our dream to see His dream come to pass, we will experience what we were created for. We can get a picture of the revelation of God's dream revealed in the prayer Jesus taught us to pray, "Your Kingdom come, Your will be done on earth as it is in heaven" (Matthew 6:10).

If heaven is to manifest itself in the earth, we will see a demonstration of the power of heaven fully attacking every work of the enemy and replacing it with God's glory, riches and purpose. This is not just a pleasant thought or idea—this was a reality in the life and ministry of Jesus.

God anointed Jesus "with the Holy Spirit and with power" (Acts 10:38). It was this anointing and miracle-working power that enabled Him to bring the presence, will and purpose of heaven to earth.

This display of power was not only to demonstrate to us how powerful He was. He was also modeling it for us because His plan was that we would also receive this anointing in His name. He promised His disciples that they would even do greater works, and He promises this to you also (see John 14:12[4]). Like Jesus, you can manifest the riches of heaven in the earth.

I love the gospels, and the book of Acts in particular, because they contain demonstrations of Kingdom power and glory. In the Bible, we read not only about Jesus performing miracles but also His disciples. The gospels and the book of Acts are full of accounts of His disciples performing the same miracles of heavenly intervention that He did.

One testimony that excites me is the miracle of the man at the Gate Beautiful (see Acts 3:1–10). Here is a man who had been lame from birth. Peter and John released "heaven on earth"—and he was healed. He began walking and leaping and praising God. The Bible says that the people who witnessed this "were filled with wonder and amazement at what had happened to him" (verse 10).

I remember a similar miracle when I was ministering in Africa years ago. A father brought his little girl to us for prayer. She was perhaps four or five years of age, but she had never walked. He showed us her legs and they were twisted and deformed from birth.

To be honest, I did not have a lot of faith at the moment. I knew Jesus was well able to do it, but I doubted that He could work such a miracle through me. I was, however, filled with compassion for both the father and the little girl. So motivated by love and out of simple obedience to the Word, I laid my hands on her and believed for a creative miracle.

She began immediately to smile and squirm, muttering something to her father in her native language. He put her down on the floor, and her legs were perfectly straight! She began to walk around the room without effort or strain; it was as if she had always walked. Her father was weeping and praising God. He was jumping up and down with ecstatic joy. Heaven's riches touched that family that day: "On earth as it is in heaven."

Jesus lived in the realm of heaven while on the earth. He brought the riches of heaven with Him everywhere He went. The blind saw, the mute spoke, the deaf heard, the lepers were cleansed, the demonized were set free and the hungry were fed.

What about you? Would you like to live in this realm? You can—God dreams about you doing this very thing! Are you willing to fulfill His dream? If you are willing, He is able!

The Divine Exchange

Jesus went to the cross and gave His life for us. He exchanged our cursed life for a blessed one. He became sin so that we would become His righteousness. He became poor so that we would be rich. He endured pain so that we would be healed. He paid the penalty for our sin in hell and was raised triumphant as He overcame all the works of the devil. Death, hell and the grave have been fully conquered through Christ. Jesus is ruler over all forever. He is the King of kings and the Lord of lords. He ascended to the right hand of the Father and gave us His Spirit so that we would exercise His authority and bring heaven to earth.

No one has to live in torment or oppression. No one has to live in bondage or lack. We can live on earth as it is in heaven. That is how Jesus taught us to pray.

All of the riches of heaven have your name on them. Christ accomplished everything needed to bring you into the fullness of all you were created for. I want to invite you to dream about the possibility of the riches of heaven filling your life and flowing through you to others in the world you live in. All things are possible, so dream big. Dream about laying hold of all the riches in glory and living in the earth as it is heaven. You are well able to access the riches of heaven: This is what you were created for.

Do you wonder why so many believers fail to access the riches of heaven or minister the blessings of heaven in the earth? Follow me into the next chapter as we look at hindrances that keep us from accessing these glorious blessings.

SUMMARY

1. God's original intent was for people to live in a heavenly atmosphere and environment filled with His presence and every good thing.
2. Human beings were created to rule and have dominion over the earth while living in harmonious fellowship with God.
3. Due to the fall of humankind into sin, the devil became the god of this world and ruled over them. The earth was then subject to darkness, oppression and evil.
4. God's plan from before the foundation of the world was to redeem the human race through Christ and restore us to relationship with God and our heavenly state. The Son of God became man and came to earth to redeem us and destroy the works of the devil.
5. Jesus preached the Kingdom of heaven and modeled the Kingdom.
6. Jesus fulfilled all righteousness and established His eternal authority through His death on the cross.

7. Jesus gave power to His people to do His works and even greater ones.
8. God's dream is for His Kingdom to come and His will to be done on earth as it is in heaven. This is to be fulfilled by His people.

QUESTIONS TO PONDER

1. What areas of your life need the manifestation of the riches of heaven?
2. What would those areas look like if they were adjusted into heavenly alignment?
3. God's intent is for you to be His instrument to bring heaven to earth—how can you see Him using you?

MAKE THIS DECLARATION OVER YOUR LIFE

Jesus, I position myself in alignment with You for Your Kingdom to come and for Your will to be done in my life on earth as it is in heaven. I am committed to seeing Your dream fulfilled. I thank You for Your finished work on the cross to secure me in Your Kingdom with all its blessings. I believe that You have filled me with the Holy Spirit and power, and that I am anointed to do the works You did in the Bible—and even greater works because You have gone to the Father. I am called and committed to manifest the Kingdom of heaven in the earth for Your glory.

2

Hindrances to Accessing the Riches of Heaven

> And it will be said, "Build up, build up, prepare the way, remove every obstacle out of the way of My people."
>
> Isaiah 57:14

I love watching crime shows. Frequently in a program the police or federal agents need to get into a building in order to investigate. On one particular episode, the federal agents approached the receptionist in a business office to access a vault, but they did not have a search warrant, so they were not given permission. They called the judge and obtained the warrant, but they continued to be hindered because the receptionist, who was the only one left in the building, told them she did not have the access code to the vault. She informed them that they would need to have the manager either disclose the code or open it for them. There was important evidence contained in the vault, but they could not obtain it due to the hindrances. Well, as in most crime shows, they found a way to gain access as they moved every hindrance out of the way and by means of a dramatic explosion blew the vault open.

Believers often suffer frustration when they fail to access God's riches of heaven. Before we move too far into sharing with you the "how-to's" of accessing these wonderful promises and encounters, let's examine the hindrances that many Christians face in encountering these glorious riches, so that we can get them out of the way.

1. Lack of Revelation

Years ago, I received a revelation from Ephesians 2:6: "and raised us up with Him, and seated us with Him in the heavenly places in Christ Jesus." I had probably read that Scripture hundreds of times previously, but on that particular day it was as if light from heaven entered my heart as I saw the reality of what it declared. Now more than just a nice concept or pleasant words—it became living truth to my heart! That same day, other Scriptures such as Colossians 1:1–3 and Hebrews 12:22–24 were also quickened to my understanding; they confirmed the position, access and entrance believers have in the heavenly dimension (more on this subject later in the book). A portal[1] of revelation from heaven had opened to me and I was enjoying revelation that flooded my being. More and more confirming Scriptures disclosed revelation over the next two days. Not only had

I received divine revelation, but when I acted on it, I experienced divine, heavenly encounters—angelic appearances, open visions and miracles. My joy was hard to contain, and I shared with everyone who would listen. I was so excited I wanted to tell the whole world that they could live their lives from a heavenly position, perspective and presence.

I pulled together the revelations about how believers have access into heavenly encounter (along with other insights concerning the glory realm) and began teaching it wherever I went to minister. One evening after I finished a session, a precious gentleman addressed me soberly and sternly, "Sister Patricia, I am very concerned about your teaching tonight." I was a little alarmed, so I asked what he meant. He explained, "You taught people that they are seated in heavenly places as though they really are." I agreed, "Yes sir, that's right, it is right here in Ephesians 2:6. That is exactly what I taught." He responded kindly but firmly, "But dear Sister Patricia, that is not real, it is simply positional theology."

I told him that I was not a theologian and at that time did not understand what he meant by positional theology. He stumbled a little as he tried to communicate what it meant and finally spit out, "Well, it's your *position*."

I excitedly replied, "That's right—exactly—it is our position! We are seated in heavenly places!" He argued, "No, no, my dear, that does not mean in reality." That really confused me. It is our position but not really? I showed him the Scripture in black and white and reiterated, "See; we *are* already seated in heavenly places in Christ—we have access through our faith." He then responded with an emphatic, "I just do not see that!"

He was being honest; he really could not grasp it. I gently responded, "Well, if you can't perceive it, you cannot have it, but I do perceive it, and I have it." He went away perplexed and frustrated. I felt bad for him because I knew he did not yet have the revelation that would "turn on the lights." I prayed for him that night that he would receive insight from the Lord so he could enjoy all God had for him.

Jesus faced similar situations in His ministry when topics He taught offended the religious leaders who were listening from a position of academic understanding. In the Kingdom, you learn by revelation that comes from the living Word and the Spirit of God.

That is why Paul prayed for those he was mentoring to receive a spirit of wisdom and revelation in the knowledge of Christ (see Ephesians 1:17). Lack of revelation of the truth will hinder your access to the riches of heaven.

Pray for revelation, that God will open your heart to grant you divine insight and understanding.

2. Wrong Core Beliefs

Your core beliefs are the concepts, insights, and knowledge you have embraced and believed with all your heart (see Proverbs 23:7). For example, if you are a carpenter and you believe with deep conviction that a hammer and nails are the only way to fasten a board, then you will not be open to using a nail gun, staples or screws. These will not be options for you because of your established, unwavering convictions.

Core beliefs must be congruent with the truth of God's Word. When I began teaching the Body of Christ how to access the riches in the heavenly dimensions of the Kingdom of God, many strongly opposed the idea that believers could experience these realms at all. Some individuals and groups even believed that anyone engaging in such practices was probably operating under the influence of witchcraft spirits.

Obviously, if you believe accessing heaven is demonic or you believe that God's people are not to live in the abundance of His blessings, you will be hindered from accessing both heaven and its riches.

3. Doubt and Unbelief

James 1:6 teaches that if you doubt when asking the Lord according to His will, you will receive nothing from the Lord and you will be unstable in all your ways. In order to experience the riches of heaven, you must believe and not doubt.

Israel doubted the Lord's promises regarding His commitment to bring them into a land flowing with milk and honey. His promises were sure, but they doubted and eventually lapsed into total unbelief. Their unbelief turned treacherous when the spies went in to scout out the Promised Land. They saw that the land was good and there was great fruit, but they came back with a bad report, saying the giants and obstacles in the land were too powerful to overcome. In contrast, Joshua and Caleb believed they could conquer with the Lord at their side, even though they saw the same giants.

As a result of their unbelief, the fearful Israelites did not enter the Promised Land, but Joshua and Caleb were not disqualified by unbelief. They believed. Therefore, when the time came, they entered the land of promise.

Unbelief hinders and often will completely block you from living in God's riches. It is actually a severe disqualifying sin in God's eyes:

> Take care, brethren, that there not be in any one of you an evil, unbelieving heart that falls away from the living God. But encourage one another day after day, as long as it is still called "Today," so that none of you will be hardened by the deceitfulness of sin. For we have become partakers of Christ, if we hold fast the beginning of our assurance firm until the end, while it is said, "Today if you hear His voice, do not harden your hearts, as when they provoked Me."
>
> For who provoked Him when they had heard? Indeed, did not all those who came out of Egypt led by Moses? And with whom was He angry for forty years? Was it not with those who sinned, whose bodies fell in the wilderness? And to whom did He swear that they would not enter His rest, but to those who were disobedient?
>
> Hebrews 3:12–18

4. Failed Attempts from the Past

Everyone experiences situations in their journey with the Lord that challenge their faith in God and their own ability to secure God's will. Perhaps you believed for someone to be healed and they died, or you prayed for a prodigal son to return to the Lord and instead he went deeper into sin, or you applied for your dream job believing you would be chosen for it and you were not. Perhaps you have gone to the altar numerous times to receive the gift of tongues[2] only to experience no manifestation of the gift. These heartbreaking situations can shake your confidence if you are not watchful.

Years ago I received a prayer request for a nine-year-old boy who was battling leukemia. He had gone through regimens of intense chemotherapy and other treatments, but the disease continued to progress aggressively. The doctors finally informed the family that his disease was terminal and there was nothing more they could do for him medically. Both the parents and the child had been in faith for his healing from the very onset. They had sought the Lord for possible roots to the infirmity, including personal and generational iniquity. They had fasted, prayed and gone through numerous deliverance and inner healing sessions, but still no breakthrough. My heart broke for them!

I rallied my intercessors and we joined them in fasting, prayer and night watches, with no success. We visited the boy and his family numerous times, sitting at his bedside, praying and confessing the Word over him day and night, without seeing results. It was heartbreaking, to say the least. He was such a sweet, precious little boy, so innocent and pure. He maintained a positive outlook and kept his faith all the way through. He never doubted and never complained.

The night he passed is still embedded in my memory. He died with peace and tranquility radiating from his little face. Yes, he was in the arms of Jesus and he no longer suffered—but how did we fail? What could we have done that we had not already done with sincere faith? Why did our faith in God's promises not produce results? His parents were in so much pain because of their loss. I had no answers; no one had answers.

Following his passing, I wrestled inside, having lost confidence in my faith. I became hesitant to pray for the sick.

We had given all we had, and it had not been enough. I was not sure that I wanted to take the emotional risk again. How could I set myself up (or those I ministered to) for another failure?

All I could do was pour my heart out to God and lay this tragedy on the altar. His Word is true. I was convinced that His love never fails, yet in this case, I had no answers. I continued to trust and not retreat, although the devil would have preferred that. I had no "Plan B." God's Word instructs us to pray for the sick, so over thirty years later I am still ministering His love and power to the sick. His Word is true.

Many dear Christians share similar stories with me. They stepped out to believe for a supernatural intervention or experience and nothing happened. Their seeming failure hinders them from stepping out again. Do not let past failures hinder you from continuing to seek the supernatural riches that are still there to be accessed. Continue to press in and believe God. Believe in God's love for you!

"Therefore, do not throw away your confidence, which has a great reward" (Hebrews 10:35).

5. Fear

I was praying for a woman to receive the gift of tongues when her body stiffened with fear, even though she had expressed a deep desire to receive this gift. Noticing the evidence of fear, I knew she would be hindered from receiving her gift.

Fear and faith cannot mix. One will cancel out the other. I stopped praying and asked the woman if she knew what was causing the fear. It took a while for her to calm down, but eventually it became clear that she was tormented by a fear of the supernatural and the unknown and was afraid of being out of control if the Spirit were to take over. Furthermore, she revealed that as a child she had had troubling spiritual experiences in nightmares; she would wake up still in the tormenting dream. This memory seemed to trigger her current reaction. I walked her through her concerns, prayed, read some Scriptures and gave her some context regarding how the Spirit would gently empower and inspire her while not controlling her or taking over her voice or physical body. She came into peace. When the fear was settled, we prayed again for her to be filled with the Spirit and speak in tongues and she received.

Many are afraid of the unknown and the spiritual dimension, but this type of tormenting fear that challenges God's truth will always hinder us from walking in all the Lord's blessings. We should consider fear to be a definite enemy to be resisted without toleration. Remember, "God has not given us a spirit of fear" (2 Timothy 1:7 NKJV).

6. Sin

Sin is lethal and will hinder us from receiving what God has for us. We exchange our sin nature for Christ's righteous nature when we are born again. This gives us righteous standing before God and has secured our inner nature (spirit man) to be without flaw, but when we choose to commit acts of sin, there are consequences. "Your iniquities have made a separation between you and God" (Isaiah 59:2). Galatians 6:7–8 says, "God is not mocked. . . .

For the one who sows to his own flesh will from the flesh reap corruption." (This word was written to born-again believers.)

Moses explains it clearly in Deuteronomy 28. Verse 12 discloses that the heavens are opened over us when we walk in obedience, while verse 23 reveals that the heavens shall become brass when we sin. If the heavens are brassed over, then the riches of heaven cannot flow into your life.

God made it easy for us to keep our slate clean and to always have a pure life so that we could live unhindered under an open heaven. 1 John 1:9 teaches us that when we confess our sins, He is faithful and righteous to forgive us and cleanse us. It is so simple. We never need to have sin hinder our access into the rich storehouse of heaven.

I suffered an emotional trauma about ten years before the writing of this book. It shook me to the core. Emotional pain, discouragement and anxiety filled me. I did the best I could to process it, but I did not take time to receive ministry and to heal. Although I was aware of the pain, my responsibilities and schedule were heavy, so I just kept moving forward. A few years later two other situations arose simultaneously that also produced emotional pain. I did the same thing as before—although I was afflicted with stress, confusion and agony of soul, I felt obligated to take care of my responsibilities and those I was serving at the time. As a result, I pushed away my own need for healing and processing and continued to move forward.

A couple of years later, I suffered some serious attacks on my health. As I sought the Lord concerning my situation, He revealed that the root was in the trauma I had experienced in my soul years earlier. I had not taken care of the fear, bitter disappointment and anxiety of the past assaults and as a result, my health was affected.

Fear, bitterness and anxiety are manifestations of sin, and the Bible teaches that anything that is not from faith is sin (see Romans 14:23[3]). I sincerely repented of the sins of fear, anxiety and bitter disappointment and received forgiveness and cleansing. Over the next week, the symptoms of the physical infirmities began to lift, and healing commenced. Sin had hindered my physical well-being because it had subtly affected areas of my emotional peace and spiritual freedom. The effects were so gradual over time that I did not recognize the full extent until years later.

Solomon was famous for his wisdom and copious wealth. God had blessed him beyond measure with favor and the manifestation of riches. But over the course of his life, he compromised and lived contrary to the Word of God by marrying foreign women, building idols to their false gods and worshipping them himself. Although God was merciful, consequences were still severe as adversaries were raised up against him and his ease of life was diminished. His sin affected his son also, as the kingdom following Solomon's death was taken from him except for one tribe, in honor of David. Sin is a cruel taskmaster. Sin hinders.

7. Lack of Focus on Truth

You empower what you focus on. Jesus taught us to be careful what we give our attention to (see Mark 4:24). Watch over the teachings you submit yourself to, the books you read and the videos you watch. What do you want measured back to you? If you focus on skepticism, the world and powerless Christianity, it will be measured back to you. If you focus on truth and holy encounters, they will be measured back to you. You empower whatever you focus on. What fills your focus?

If you are not focused on truth, it is possible you are focused on the mundane or the false. Your lack of focus on the riches available to you in heaven will disempower that realm of revelation and encounter in your life.

When I mentor believers in the matters of the Spirit, I always emphasize meditation (pondering, studying, deep thinking, imagining) on the lesson, as well as activation. It is one thing to sit through a lecture and find it interesting, but it is another thing altogether to focus on the teachings until they become part of who you are. They need to become your internal reality, and this comes through focus.

When I was in the fifth grade, I delivered a disappointing report card to my parents. They took me to the teacher to discuss my poor marks. The teacher explained that she thought I had a healthy intellect but was not focused. She said, "Patricia is constantly distracted and loses focus. Therefore, what she is learning is not being absorbed."

Well, needless to say, my parents made sure I focused on my studies following that. They set up a strict homework regimen to make sure I was learning the curriculum and then tested me on it over and over until they knew I had it. They took away my television and radio privileges until I improved. My report card for the next quarter was the best I had ever received. I just needed a little focus.

The more you study, meditate on and activate the truth of God's Word concerning the supernatural and the blessings that are awaiting you as you access the riches of heaven, the more you will enjoy the manifestations of that which you are focused on.

> How blessed is the man who does not walk in the counsel of the wicked, nor stand in the path of sinners, nor sit in the seat of scoffers! But his delight is in the law of the Lord, and in His law he meditates day and night. He will be like a tree firmly planted by streams of water, which yields its fruit in its season and its leaf does not wither; and in whatever he does, he prospers.
>
> Psalm 1:1–3

8. Lack of Expectation

Sometimes believers are hindered from receiving manifestations of God's heavenly riches because they lack expectation. Expectation is the catalyst for miracles. Let's consider blind Bartimaeus (see Mark 10:46–52).

Bartimaeus had great expectation for a miracle and he received what he was expecting. He was so expectant that he threw away his beggar's cloak. That was a big deal; in that day, only those who were legitimately infirm were allowed to have a beggar's cloak, which gave them the legal right to receive alms from passersby. Receiving alms had been his living and only means of support. Even before he was healed, he cast off his cloak. He was unlikely to be able to retrieve it after that, as many would have already grabbed for it. He took the risk because he expected his miracle.

I have discovered that many believers who say they are not receiving their breakthroughs into heavenly access often do not receive because there is a lack of expectation. This hinders your ability to receive. Stir up expectation.

9. Unhealthy Associations

My mother taught me to always choose my friends wisely as those you associate with will have influence on you for good or for "not so good." Many a child has gone wayward because of the friends they hung out with. You need to consider your associations as you are growing in the supernatural dimensions of the Kingdom.

If your friends, family and fellow church members resist the truth about your access into the riches of heaven, your faith and passion can be dampened and hindered. In Jesus' day, many followed Him, but there were also those who followed the teachings and beliefs of the religious leaders who opposed His teachings. Those who associated with Christ witnessed and experienced miracles and revelatory teachings, but those who associated with the religious leaders were hindered from coming into the knowledge of the truth; they became skeptics, persecutors and resisters of the Gospel.

I am not advocating refusing to love someone because they have hurt you or because you are moving on, but there are times when you must distance yourself somewhat from relationship with people who oppose your desire for the realm of the Spirit. Carve out some new relationships. Intentionally choose to build relationships with those who are passionate for the supernatural Kingdom of God. If you associate with prophetic people, you will become more prophetic. If you associate with people who are passionate to pursue God's glory, you will become more passionate, too. If you associate with skeptics, you will become more skeptical of everything God is doing.

10. Lack of Perseverance and Endurance

Many believers slip into a victim mentality without realizing it. In my early years as a Christian I went through a difficult season in which I felt the impact of many circumstantial pressures. I felt backed into a corner. One day I was crying out to God with all my heart. (I was actually moaning and groaning rather than praying victorious prayers.) I was trying to fight off the enemy from my little corner, attempting to keep him at bay. The Lord spoke to my heart at that moment, saying, *What are you doing playing the victim in the corner? You were not created to be a victim—you are a victor. Rise up and fight! You are not to be on the defense but on the offense. Persevere, endure, and press on through.*

I had defaulted to a defensive, victim mentality rather than being persistent in my faith, aggressively enduring until I broke through. I rose up that day and let the enemy have it with both barrels! Why play the victim in the corner when I am the victor through Christ?

Sometimes believers are not willing to fight through the resistance in order to obtain their breakthrough, so they remain in their corner, defeated. Breakthrough into new realms of supernatural experience demands some perseverance and endurance. Anything that has value is worth going after.

Paul said that he pressed on "toward the mark for the prize of the high calling of God in Christ Jesus" (Philippians 3:14 KJV). To press is to push against resistance. It is not always easy, but it is worth it. Offensive posture is important. Perseverance is important. Endurance is important. Be willing to push forward, persevere and endure. "If we endure, we will also reign with Him" (2 Timothy 2:12).

11. Negativity

Israel was supposed to enter the Promised Land by the word of the Lord, but all the way there, they constantly murmured and complained. God had given them so many glorious, supernatural graces (manna from heaven every day, water out of the rock, provision of quail, the glory cloud by day and the pillar of fire by night, the invitation to meet with Him face-to-face in the tent of meeting, etc.), but all they could see was what they did not have. They always saw their cup as half empty instead of half full. As they ate food from heaven they murmured and complained because they missed the leeks and garlic of Egypt. Because they failed to enjoy the enormous blessings of God in the wilderness, they failed to enter the Promised Land. Their negativity kept them back.

While laboring on the mission field in Belize, Central America, I served as leader of the kitchen and cooked meals three times a day for over fifty team members with a "faith budget" (I had to believe for the food). I did my very best to exercise my faith and my creativity. Our diet was low on protein (except when Jungle Joe brought home an iguana on his hunting days) and high in carbohydrates. As a result, the women gained weight and the men lost weight. None of them were happy with me, and they were constantly murmuring, grumbling and complaining about the food.

One day I was making bread—with flour from which I had extracted the bugs and larvae—weeping over the kneading bowl. I cried out to God, asking Him what was blocking the provision of food. He showed me that the negativity, murmuring and complaining had "brassed over the heavens." As a group, we repented and began to rejoice with thanksgiving in God's goodness and all He had for us. Within twenty-four hours of our repentance and change of attitude, the heavens opened and miracle food provision was released. From that time on, the blessing of abundant provision of food never stopped!

Negativity, murmuring and complaining hinder you from accessing the full riches of heaven.

12. Warfare and Demonic Resistance

The New Testament teaches us how to withstand warfare and defeat the enemy. Peter warns believers regarding the tactics of the enemy: "Be of sober spirit, be on the alert. Your adversary, the devil, prowls around like a roaring lion, seeking someone to devour" (1 Peter 5:8).

Paul also addressed spiritual warfare as he taught the church at Ephesus:

> Put on the full armor of God, so that you will be able to stand firm against the schemes of the devil. For our struggle is not against flesh and blood, but against the rulers, against the powers, against the world forces of this darkness, against the spiritual forces of wickedness in the heavenly places. Therefore, take up the full armor of God, so that you will be able to resist in the evil day, and having done everything, to stand firm.
>
> Ephesians 6:11–13

When you are pursuing supernatural engagement with heaven, you can be assured that the enemy of your soul will attempt to discourage you from moving forward. If you fall into the snare of his deceptions and schemes, you will certainly be hindered from moving forward. His usual tactics are to bring accusation or condemnation toward you or to hinder you through distracting circumstances. Most of the time, you engage the enemy on the battlefield of your mind.

When I was learning to prophesy, I had been taught by my mentor to take every opportunity to activate the prophetic, so I did. Every Bible study and prayer meeting I went to, I stepped out in faith to prophesy. One evening I attended a Bible study in my neighborhood. During worship, I came under prophetic unction and delivered a word at the appropriate time. Immediately, thoughts of accusation came into my mind: *Who do you think you are? You are so off! You have no right to prophesy!* Those words plagued me all week. For seven days, the devil targeted me with condemnation, shame and guilt. When the enemy attacks, he usually speaks into your mind and the messages you hear often feel like your own thoughts even though they originate with him.

I attended the meeting the next week and again delivered a prophetic word. The same warfare hit me. My thoughts rallied against me: *They hate you at that Bible study. The words you bring there are false. You are an imposter. You are a loser.* I cried many times that week under the emotional impact and weight of the accusation.

I decided that I was never going to prophesy again! I was not going to attend the prayer meeting and Bible study again. However, when the evening came around for the scheduled meeting, I felt a gentle nudge from the Spirit to attend. I strongly resisted it, but the nudge would not go away. The last place I wanted to be was at that Bible study. I felt so much shame and I had lost my confidence. Although I tried to resist, the Spirit won the call and off I went to the meeting. I arrived late and did not prophesy. I could hardly wait to leave, so I slipped out as early as possible. As I was on my way out to the parking lot, one of the leaders came running after me. He said, "Patricia, just a minute. We have all been talking about you and your prophetic ministry this week."

My heart sank—*Oh no, now I am going to get it!*

He continued, "We have been so blessed and amazed by the accuracy of your prophetic words and they have had great impact on us. Could you teach us what you know about the prophetic?" No one was more shocked than I was. I had almost never prophesied again because of some stupid warfare assault from the enemy. My life in Christ and my ministry to the Body could have been completely blocked because of warfare.

The devil is a liar. He will always want you to retreat but Jesus has given you "power . . . over all the power of the enemy!" (Luke 10:19 NKJV).

What are the things that have hindered you in the past? Identify them and be determined to have your breakthrough. God says, "Move on forward without hindrance into the fullness of all I have for you." In the next chapter, I will introduce you to the Treasury Room in heaven and the abundant life that you have been given through Christ. You will love it!

SUMMARY

Believers suffer frustration and failure to access God's riches of heaven due to hindrances such as these:

1. **Lack of revelation.** Revelation—divine insight and understanding to grasp His spiritual truths, secrets and treasures—comes from the living Word and the Spirit of God. You need to "see" it in order to have it.
2. **Wrong core beliefs.** These are the concepts, insights and knowledge you have embraced and believed in your heart. Core beliefs must be congruent with the truth of God's Word in order to access all He has for you.
3. **Doubt and unbelief.** Unbelief hinders and may completely block you from living in the fulfillment of God's heavenly riches. It is actually a severe disqualifying sin in God's eyes.
4. **Failed attempts from the past.** Do not let past failures or attempts to step out in faith hinder you. Continue to press in and believe.
5. **Fear.** Many are afraid of the unknown spiritual dimension, and such fear will always hinder you from acquiring and walking in all the blessings the Lord has for you. Fear is an enemy to be resisted without toleration.
6. **Sin.** Sin is lethal and will hinder you from receiving what God has for you. The Bible teaches that when we walk in obedience, the heavens are opened to us, but when we sin, they become like brass.
7. **Lack of focus on the truth.** Lack of focus on the riches available to you in heaven will disempower that realm

of revelation and encounter in your life. What you focus on, you empower.

8. **Lack of expectation.** Expectation is the catalyst for miracles and receiving manifestations of God's heavenly riches. If you are lacking expectation, stir it up!
9. **Unhealthy associations.** If the people around you resist the truth about your access into heaven's riches, your faith and passion can be dampened. Intentionally build relationships with those who are passionate for the supernatural Kingdom of God.
10. **Lack of perseverance and endurance.** Breakthrough into new realms of supernatural experience demands perseverance and endurance. Anything that has value is worth going after. Be willing to push forward.
11. **Negativity.** Negativity, murmuring and complaining hinder you from accessing heavens riches. Live a life of joyful thanksgiving for God's goodness and all He has done.
12. **Warfare and demonic resistance.** When you are pursuing engagement in the supernatural, you can be assured that the enemy of your soul will attempt to hinder and discourage you. Do not listen to his lies—resist and move forward!

QUESTIONS TO PONDER

1. What hindrances in this chapter do you relate to?
2. Which hindrance do you believe is your greatest obstacle to encountering God's promises for your life?
3. What are some actions you can take to remove those hindrances?

MAKE THIS DECLARATION OVER YOUR LIFE

Jesus, I determine to resist everything that would attempt to hinder my encounters with You as You reveal to me Your riches in heaven. I am open to all You desire to show me in Your Word and all You desire to give me in the realm of encounters. With great expectation I look forward to experiencing You and Your goodness.

3

Heaven's Abundant Life

> In My Father's house are many dwelling places; if it were not so, I would have told you; for I go to prepare a place for you.
>
> John 14:2

On April 6, 2018, in Detroit, Michigan, during a worship service, I was blessed with an extraordinary encounter in the Treasury Room of heaven. While I was in deep worship, the Spirit of God led me into a real-life spiritual experience where I stood at the entrance of a room in heaven with double doors opened wide. I heard the Lord beckoning me to enter. He did not speak in an audible voice; rather, clear and tender thoughts were spoken into my heart. As I stepped over the threshold, I was speechless with awe. The walls, ceiling and floor of this room were constructed with what appeared to be pure gold that emanated pulsating life and light. The gold was so pure you could see through it, and it seemed to go on forever. Glory filled the atmosphere. In the center of the room stood a crimson wooden treasure chest filled with golden coins. The chest and the coins were pulsating with light and life. Everything was dazzling—there are no words to describe the glory of it all.

But as beautiful and glorious as this sight was, everything paled in comparison to the One who stood in the midst of this room. Standing behind and to the side of the treasure chest was Jesus Himself. He was wrapped in a glistening light-radiating robe. Everything about Him radiated authority and created an awe-saturated atmosphere. His eyes were rich sapphire in color and His face shone with a warm love-glow that filled the room. I wept as I beheld Him. There is nothing in life that compares to Him. He is the treasure! When you behold Him, you have truly found eternitiy's treasure.

Heaven is a very real place, the location of God's abode. Jesus taught that in heaven are many realms or specific dwelling places. He further taught His disciples that through His death on the cross and resurrection, He was making a way for them (and all believers) to be where He is. He implied that when He came back to them following His resurrection, the way would have been finalized for them/us to have full access into this glorious abode of God with all of its dwelling places:

> In My Father's house are many dwelling places; if it were not so, I would have told you; for I go to prepare a place for you. If I go and prepare a place for you, I will come again and receive you to Myself, that where I am, there you may be also.
>
> John 14:2–3

Many believers do not understand that heaven is available for us to access and experience while we still live in the earth. Jesus revealed to us that in His earthly ministry, He did only the things He saw His Father do (John 5:19), but He also taught in Matthew 6:9 that His Father lives in heaven, so Jesus must have had access into heaven in order to see what His Father was doing so He could replicate it on the earth. Jesus lived in awareness of two realms simultaneously, the heavenly and the earthly (bilocation).

Jesus further explained this reality of experiencing two realms at the same time to a religious scholar, Nicodemus, who had been struggling with the spiritual concept of being born again.

> If I have told you earthly things and you do not believe, how will you believe if I tell you heavenly things? No one has ascended to heaven but He who came down from heaven, that is, the Son of Man who is in heaven.
>
> John 3:12–13 NKJV

He was speaking with Nicodemus while in the earth. Both He and Nicodemus were standing on earthly soil, but He clearly explained that He was in heaven also: "That is the Son of Man who *is* in heaven."

The apostle Paul also alludes to this positional bilocation of believers in his letter to the Ephesians:

> I pray that the eyes of your heart may be enlightened, so that you will know what is the hope of His calling, what are the riches of the glory of His inheritance in the saints, and what is the surpassing greatness of His power toward us who believe. These are in accordance with the working

> of the strength of His might which He brought about in Christ, when He raised Him from the dead and seated Him at His right hand in the heavenly places, far above all rule and authority and power and dominion, and every name that is named, not only in this age but also in the one to come. And He put all things in subjection under His feet, and gave Him as head over all things to the church, which is His body, the fullness of Him who fills all in all.
>
> Ephesians 1:18–23

> But God, being rich in mercy, because of His great love with which He loved us, even when we were dead in our transgressions, made us alive together with Christ (by grace you have been saved), and raised us up with Him, and seated us with Him in the heavenly places in Christ Jesus.
>
> Ephesians 2:4–6

According to these Scriptures, we are already seated in heavenly places in Christ if He lives in our heart as Savior and Lord. Jesus gave us access, and that is why all believers can enjoy encounters in the heavenly places while they are still living in the earth. This is not just for a few specially appointed people in the church; this is for all who believe the truth regarding these realities and enter by faith, led by the Spirit. As a believer in Christ, you are no longer an earthly being trying to get into heaven—you are a heavenly being living on the earth!

Jesus Is Abundant Life

The Treasury Room is a place in heaven where the riches of Christ can be found, but it is not so much about the room or the riches as it is about the One who stands in the midst of this—and every—room in heaven. Jesus is the center of all life and the central focus of all that is in heaven and earth. He is everything you need. When you have Him, you have access to all the riches of heaven. He *is* the glory. He *is* your provision. He is everything!

Jesus wants you to know Him—His thoughts, His ways, His glory and His Word. He longs for every believer to live an abundant and full life, overflowing with God's goodness. His teachings in the gospels confirm this: "The thief comes only to steal and kill and destroy; I came that they may have life, and have it abundantly" (John 10:10).

Jesus did not come to give us a life filled with lack, poverty and misery. He not only came to give us life in its abundance, He *is* abundant life (see John 14:6[1]).

A few years back, a very well-educated Christian leader challenged me on my belief regarding living an abundantly blessed life filled with the treasures of heaven. He said, "I believe you are blessed when you are poor, and God wants His people to embrace suffering." He then proceeded to expound on his beliefs with numerous theological confirmations from his academic studies, attempting to persuade me to believe that God even intentionally afflicts people with poverty, sickness and tragedy so they can learn to be blessed in their sufferings.

I stood a little shocked and inquired of him, "Do you believe there is poverty, lack, sickness and suffering in heaven?" He answered a definite "no." I confirmed that Jesus taught us to pray to the Father, "Your kingdom come, Your will be done, on earth as it is in heaven" (Matthew 6:10). Jesus also taught and declared that He came to give us life in its abundance; it is the enemy who steals, kills and destroys.

At the end of our conversation we agreed to disagree but my conviction to preach Christ's gospel of *abundant life* intensified greatly as a result of that dialogue. Jesus came to destroy the works of the evil one, not to empower them (see 1 John 3:8).

When you receive Jesus as your Savior, you have His life living in you. His life in you is eternal life, pure life, good life, glorious life, rich life—*abundant life*! You are walking around with abundant life within. You are a container for His life and you can have that life spilling out into all that pertains to you and to everyone around you.

Heaven has no lack—only abundance of provision, health, peace, joy and love. The very atmosphere of heaven is filled with the abundance of all things and Jesus is the very source of that abundant life. He is your access into the abundance of heavenly places, so it is important to honor and desire Him above all else. Heavenly riches such as material provision, health, strength, wisdom, power, blessed relationships, righteousness, talents and gifting are all part of the "love-package" He gives freely to all who believe in Him. Jesus is so extravagantly generous that He gives us every heavenly blessing and every earthly blessing. Everything that one needs to live an abundant and blessed life was already given to you two thousand years ago through Christ's finished work on the cross. And the good news is that these blessings are for every believer, and that includes you! Jesus is both the treasure and the distributor to His people of the abundant riches of heaven:

> Blessed be the God and Father of our Lord Jesus Christ, who has blessed us with every spiritual blessing in the heavenly places in Christ.
>
> Ephesians 1:3

> [Jesus'] divine power has granted to us everything pertaining to life and godliness, through the true knowledge of Him who called us by His own glory and excellence. For by these He has granted to us His precious and magnificent promises, so that by them you may become partakers of the divine nature, having escaped the corruption that is in the world by lust.
>
> 2 Peter 1:3–4

What great treasures: every blessing in heaven and every blessing that pertains to life and godliness in the earth! That is mega-extravagance! Many, however, have more passion to pursue these aspects of abundant life than they do Christ Himself. Abundant life includes all those blessings, but again, we must remember that abundant life is a Person. God wants you to have all things in abundance and He has given you all things through the eternal covenant Christ secured for you on the cross, but He wants you always to put things in the right priority.

We live in a world whose message and marketing are constantly declaring that our fulfillment and success in life will be as a result of the worldly possessions we acquire. This is so far from the truth. We can never truly be rich if we do not understand that "God + Nothing = Everything We Need." The "stuff" can follow and be added to us, but the heart and center of it all is Christ.

Our family was living in Central America on a mission assignment back in the early 1980s. Our two sons were young, ages seven and nine, and we were living by faith with no visible means of support. Two and a half years earlier, we had left our careers and secular employment in order to pursue the call of God on our lives. It was a difficult season as we were learning how to live on His promises by faith. Our life on the mission field was simple and extremely lean. Our housing consisted of a small two-bedroom house shared with another family. Our meals were basic: mainly rice and beans . . . and beans and rice. We definitely did not experience any Western flare or extravagance in areas of food, lodging, clothing, and finance, and yet there was abundance to be found if we just looked for it. We had so much to be thankful for. However, during this learning curve of living by faith, at times I often looked at what we did not have rather than what we did have.

While sitting one morning in a gazebo, I was pouring out my complaints before the Lord—mainly regarding the lack of funds. Our life on the mission field was challenging, and I had just gone to the mailbox, hoping for a "check in the mail" or some other means of financial support, as we had absolutely no money. But to my great disappointment, the mailbox was empty, and I was heartbroken. This was not unusual as many weeks would go by with no letters or support, but that particular morning I really needed a sign of breakthrough.

As I sought the Lord's presence and wisdom that day, He revealed to me that my provision was in Him and not in the mailbox. The mailbox was not my source—He was. He further revealed to me that the abundant life is not about money—abundant life is about Him. Every good and perfect gift comes from Him.

When God's people were in the wilderness, they did not need money to buy bread—He rained it down upon them from heaven. It was fresh every morning and they could eat to the full. They did not need money to buy water—He supplied it out of a rock. They did not need money to be entertained—God invited them to meet with Him in the Tent of Meeting whenever they wanted. Their clothing did not wear out for the entire forty years. They did not need money for medical bills because God was the God who healed them and He kept them in health. They lived in abundance! I realized that day, in the gazebo in Central America, that we also lived in abundance even though earthly currency was lean. There was not a day when we were without His presence, food, clothing and transportation. His goodness and provision could be found every day. I had lost sight of the fact that Jesus Himself was my treasure.

Later that day, the Lord gave me a confirmation to my divine adjustment. My youngest son came running into the kitchen where I was sitting on a wooden stool, sifting weevils out of the rice.

"Mommy, God gave me a really good day today," he eagerly shared.

"What did God do for you today?" I asked, as I put aside the rice bowl, picked him up and set him on my lap.

"We caught a tarantula and fed it to the chickens"! He breathlessly explained how cool it was to watch the chickens attack the spider, devouring it for their breakfast. He then shared how he and his friends had gone swimming in the nearby creek and on the way back saw a boa constrictor that Jungle Joe had just killed and later put in the freezer. In the afternoon they went to our friend's ranch and visited his pet baby jaguar. He could not stop talking about his eventful day and he knew with innocent faith that it was God Himself who had made it glorious. I am not a fan of spiders and snakes but I put on the happy face for him as it was one of the best days in his life to that point. In his perspective, it was full and abundant. God had placed special treasures in that day just for him and they could not be bought for a price. Although he is now in his forties, he still remembers with fondness days like that. He enjoyed his amazing life on the mission field.

As I reflect today on that season, I do not remember the hardships. I remember only the fond memories of the goodness of God. I remember the people that we reached with the Gospel, those who came to Christ, those who were healed and delivered. Many of the most challenging moments have become some of the best stories to share as I preach. God truly gives us life-giving eternal treasures from the difficult seasons of our life:

> I will give you the treasures of darkness and hidden wealth of secret places, so that you may know that it is I, the Lord, the God of Israel, who calls you by your name.
>
> Isaiah 45:3

Abundance is so much more than having a bunch of "stuff" with which so many get weighed down, either from the anguish of not having enough or the burden of stewardship of having too much. Jesus taught:

> Do not store up for yourselves treasures on earth, where moth and rust destroy, and where thieves break in and steal. But store up for yourselves treasures in heaven, where neither moth nor rust destroys, and where thieves do not break in or steal; for where your treasure is, there your heart will be also.
>
> Matthew 6:19–21

Riches in Glory

We have established that Jesus is Abundant Life and He is the Treasure, but now let's look at an often-quoted Scripture and discover an important insight: "My God will supply all your needs according to His riches in glory in Christ Jesus" (Philippians 4:19). When believers quote this, they usually emphasize "all my needs will be met by God."

Let's read it carefully. How is God going to supply all your needs? It is according to His riches in glory in Christ. Paul points to the Treasure and the glory in Christ. Wealth—one of the meanings of glory—comes in and through Christ. Glory is also the atmosphere of heaven. All the riches and wealth of heaven are available to every believer in Christ. When you have Christ you have access to it all. This is abundant life.

Over the years I have taught many believers how to access abundant provision, healing, deliverance and breakthrough. God's love is so extravagant, you would be surprised how much He longs to give to those who seek Him. When you activate your faith to receive provision from the heavenly realm, it manifests itself in the earthly dimension.

At a Glory School we hosted in Tucson, Arizona, years ago, we were activating the students to follow the Holy Spirit as they ascended by faith into the heavens. They were to ask the Lord to reveal to them blessings in heaven that they were to receive by faith and bring back into the natural realm. After the activation, I had students share their encounters. It was wonderful to hear how God led many to receive healing, strength, restoration of relationships, anointing, salvations of loved ones and various types of provision while in their encounter. One very excited young man came forward to share. He testified that God led Him into a room in heaven and showed him his dream sports car. He was ecstatic as he shared that God told him to bring the car back into the earthly realm by faith. He had absolute assurance. To be honest with you, I was a bit concerned. I had wanted to avoid a focus on material things and I questioned within my heart why God would reveal something so lavish to this young man. Not wanting to discourage him, I kept my concerns to myself.

Within the next month, I was at another event and the same young man came running up to me with his laptop. He showed me his screen saver—a photo of a black BMW sports car sitting in a driveway. He was jumping up and down with excitement saying, "This is it! This is it! . . . Remember when I went into heaven and the Holy Spirit told me to bring the car back? . . . This is it! It is mine! . . . It is in my driveway! God gave it to me!"

I was totally amazed that God would be so extravagant with things that were not necessities, but I could see that the situations that had led up to acquiring his dream-mobile were definite evidence of God's intervention and lavish divine favor. As a result of that miracle, the young man became more grounded in his understanding of God as a good Father. I rejoiced with him.

After that event, I left for another ministry engagement in Texas. During one of the lunch breaks, I was on my way back to the venue. As I walked through the parking lot, a woman came toward me calling my name. She said, "You may not remember me, but I was at your Glory School in Tucson. When I went into heaven that day, the Holy

Spirit showed me a beautiful black car—a Jaguar—that He was giving to me. I was elated and received it by faith and brought it back into the natural realm as you taught us." She further explained, "I was going to testify about it, but then the young man got up and shared about his black sports car. I thought it was weird that God would be giving out luxury cars, so I held back." When she returned to Texas, her husband met her at the airport and drove her home. In her driveway was a brand-new black Jaguar. He had bought it for her after she had the heavenly encounter although she had not shared her experience with him or anyone else.

Needless to say, this enlarged my understanding about God's extravagant love and revealed greater insight into His glorious, generous heart. These two believers were not seeking the cars, they were following the Spirit, but God knew the desires of their heart. He loves satisfying the deepest longings of our hearts. God wants us to understand that He is committed to blessing us with everything that pertains to life—even nonessential things like automobiles.

The Treasury Room is open! It has your name on it as does everything included in Christ's abundant life. It is time for you not only to explore these awesome, glorious, treasures but to lay hold of them and bring them to earth. Jesus brought heavenly salvation, healing, deliverance, freedom and provision when He came to the earth. You too can reach out to "Christ Jesus our Lord, in whom we have boldness and confident access through faith in Him" (Ephesians 3:11–12).

In the next chapter, I will help you to discover four realms of abundance that are available to you.

SUMMARY

1. Heaven is a real place where God lives, filled with abundance and glory. He has prepared many dwelling places for us through Christ, whose finished work on the cross gave us access.
2. Jesus *is* the Treasure! Jesus is our center focus as we pursue the riches of heaven. Everything else pales in comparison to Him. God + Nothing = Everything We Need.
3. Jesus came to give life in abundance to all His children. He *is* abundant life.
4. When we are in relationship with Jesus, we have access to the abundance of heaven. Through faith, by following His Spirit, we can receive the manifestations of His abundance.

QUESTIONS TO PONDER

1. Do you consider Jesus to be the greatest treasure in your life? If not, what is your greatest treasure?
2. When you think of abundant life, what does that mean to you? If you were to live on earth with the abundance of Christ fully manifested in your life, what would that look like? Do not be afraid to imagine *big*! Remember Ephesians 3:20, which says, "To Him who is able to do far more abundantly beyond all that we ask or think, according to the power that works within us."
3. Would you enjoy experiencing the heavenly dimension?

MAKE THIS DECLARATION OVER YOUR LIFE

Jesus, You are my treasure and I love You more than life itself. You meet all my needs according to Your riches in glory and have blessed me beyond measure with abundant life now and forever. As a heavenly being living on the earth, I experience the heavenly realm by faith and I lay hold of Your promises with bold access before Your throne of grace.

4

Four Realms of Abundance

> I came that they may have life, and have it abundantly.
>
> John 10:10

On October 29, 2013, I was in my kitchen making breakfast for some house guests we were hosting during a ten-day tent revival that our ministry was co-facilitating. Suddenly an angel appeared with three scrolls, each of which contained a message regarding the future. I stood in awe, with both tears and laughter, in the midst of the encounter. When my guests came down into the kitchen for breakfast, I shared the encounter with them and they too were blessed and filled with expectation.

As we drove to the tent revival, we were already revived for sure. The more we reflected on the visitation, the more

God's glory surrounded us. By the time I arrived at the meeting, I was ready to engage in worship with all my heart. The three words that the angel brought were already great treasures from heaven, but during heartfelt worship, the Lord gave me a fourth word, this time not delivered by an angel but by the Spirit of God speaking to my heart.

The Lord quickened a Scripture to my mind. I looked it up right away to make sure I remembered the details correctly. The Scripture revealed four realms of abundance that God desires to bless all His people with:

> Now Isaac sowed in that land and reaped in the same year a hundredfold. And the Lord blessed him, and the man became rich, and continued to grow richer until he became very wealthy.
>
> Genesis 26:12–13

I will break down for you the four levels or realms of abundance, which are being offered to you—yes, I mean *you*—in every area of your life.

Let's look at the definition of the word "realm": (1) A royal domain, a kingdom such as the "realm of England." A region someone has dominion or rule over. (2) The region, sphere or domain within which anything occurs, prevails or dominates, such as the "realm of dreams."

When you live in a "realm" you live in an established sphere of influence where you have dominion, authority and experience.

Later in the chapter, I will share some insights on how to build and carve out a realm, but first, let's look at the four realms of abundance that are offered you in Christ.

Realm #1: Reaping the harvest that you have sown

"Now Isaac sowed in that land and reaped in the same year a hundredfold." There had been a famine in the land, so God told Isaac to go to Gerar, the land of the Philistines. He was obedient to God because he believed in the covenant of blessing God had made with his father, Abraham. Knowing that God would be with Him, he sowed seed in faith, confident that he would reap. As a result, he reaped one hundredfold in the same year that he sowed.

This realm of harvest is available to you. Imagine your life full and overflowing with every good thing you have ever sown. That would be exciting. But you cannot reap a harvest you do not sow.

God made a perpetual covenant with man: "While the earth remains, seedtime and harvest, and cold and heat, and summer and winter, and day and night shall not cease" (Genesis 8:22). In other words, as long as the earth remains there will be a corresponding harvest to every seed you sow.

The morning God spoke the word regarding Isaac and the four realms of abundance, I became very excited, filled with faith and expectancy when I noted that Isaac reaped "a hundredfold" in the same year. How much is that? Some commentaries explain that this means one hundred times as much, but other commentaries teach that it is "folded over" one hundred times. In other words, $1.00 folded over would be $2.00, which folded over would be $4.00, which folded over would be $8.00, which folded over would be $16.00, etc. An amount folded over one hundred times yields a massive increase. Either way you calculate it, God's economy is amazing!

Our ministry at the time was working on a project for which we still needed $100,000 to complete. The spirit of faith filled me and I took my bankbook out to write a donation check for $1,000. My expectation was that it would increase to the $100,000 our ministry needed. Joy filled my heart. Unable to wait for the scheduled offering time, I ran up immediately to the platform and put it in the offering bucket, returning to my seat in great excitement. The day I gave that donation was October 29, 2013, two months before the end of the year. I decreed over my offering that one hundred times would be returned *before* the end of the year, and it was.

The $100,000 came in less than three weeks later. *And* my husband and I received a personal blessing, too. We had been waiting for a $200,000 investment to come through that had been stalled since August and it came into our hands at the same time. *And* our ministry continued to be blessed with weekly abundance after that seed had been planted; it was a seed that just kept on producing!

The Power of Intentionality

The principle of sowing and reaping is easy to see in natural life. A farmer, for example, will look at the land he has available and intentionally calculate the crop he desires to reap. He chooses what type of crop he wants and how much yield to expect. Once he calculates that, he determines what type of seed he needs to sow and how much seed to plant to get his expected yield. He then sows with focused intention to obtain his anticipated harvest.

Those in the business world are very familiar with the principle of sowing and reaping concerning investments. They know that they must make an investment first in order to obtain an increase. No investment means no increase—it is that simple. They also research the project or business before investing. Investors calculate their estimated return based on what their investment can potentially yield, always with an intention to receive back more than their initial investment.

For some reason many believers struggle with the whole concept of sowing and reaping, although it is what Kingdom economy is based on. This principle applies not only to financial return but also to every area of our lives. It is so simple: Whatever you sow, you will reap.

I have heard Christians say, "I do not sow a financial gift into a ministry in order to get anything back; I just sow it in love for the Lord." Although I admire the heart that gives in full abandonment without selfish motive, it is not the Lord's will for us to just throw money out there. That would be like a farmer saying, "I just love the Lord and I know that He is the One who has supplied the seed, so I do not need a return, I just love to throw the seed into the field because of my love for Him. I do not expect increase." Honestly, that farmer would not be in the agricultural business for long! Once his seed was used up, there would be no more harvest unless he went out and intentionally reaped what he had sown and used the increase to sow again. Every harvest gives you opportunity to increase. Some of your harvest is for your benefit and some is folded back into further sowing and reaping.

When the Lord first called me to labor in the field of rescuing children from sex trafficking in Cambodia in 2010, I realized that one of the main reasons parents sold their children into the industry was because of systemic poverty. The traffickers would entice the parents by saying that they could buy one of their many children in order to make one less mouth to feed, and they offered a little cash to pay for the rest of the family's supply of rice for the month. The traffickers would lie, promising to take the children to rich families in Thailand where they could grow up in wealthy homes and get schooled. Later, they lied, the children could return and look after their families. This motivated the parents to sell their children, thinking they were helping their children and their family. But it was not true. Their children were sold into sex slavery. (Note: There is more awareness now, but some parents are still selling their children for money even though they realize what is happening to them.)

The Lord revealed many ways for us to intentionally counteract the trafficking of the children. One of the ways was to establish businesses in the villages among the poor, so they would not need to sell their children. The first business was Purity Laundry Services. We began that business by intentionally sowing a bag of soap, two basins and some clothespins. (We also purchased an electric washer but they never used it; they preferred to wash the clothes by hand.) Before long our little bag of soap and basins had increased to not only cover enough for more laundry supplies but also to fund three families in the slums. Purity Laundry Services has grown and is still a flourishing business in Cambodia.

Our next business was King's Crown Jewelry. Someone had donated a bag of beads to our ministry. We approached a young couple who had no means of support and asked them if they wanted their own business. We taught them how to make jewelry, intentionally sowing the bag of beads and purchasing some other supplies for them to get started. In the very first month they earned more income than they had ever made in their lives. We taught them how to reinvest into more supplies to build their business. Within a couple of months, they were supporting others whom they hired into the company.

I taught my sons when they were young to intentionally sow in order to reap. Desire friends? Sow friendship. Desire kindness? Sow kindness, etc. Intentional sowing brings forth a harvest.

In the parable about the sower and the seed (see Mark 4:1–20), Jesus thoroughly covered this principle. He taught that when you sow into good ground, you are promised a thirty-, sixty-, even a hundredfold return. He explained that the seed is the Word of God. When you intentionally sow the Word into a situation, it will yield a proportionate harvest, but the principle here is not limited to sowing the Word only.

Jesus Himself sowed His life in order to reap a harvest for all eternity. He intentionally sowed His life through His death on the cross and as a result, He reaped you and everyone who ever receives Him as their Savior. Eternity will be filled with the harvest of the life He sowed.

Sowing and reaping is a spiritual exercise. When you sow in the earth by faith, heaven blesses the seed and brings forth increase.

Reaping Promises

Whenever you read a promise in the Word, you can sow into it. For example, Malachi 3:10–12 is loaded with promises concerning the tithe[1]. The tithe is a clear key to accessing the blessings of heaven. All the promises regarding the tithe are the fruit you can harvest if you sow the seed of your tithe to God in the field He instructs. If you sow according to His instruction, you will reap the harvest promised.

> "Bring the whole tithe into the storehouse, so that there may be food in My house, and test Me now in this," says the LORD of hosts, "if I will not open for you the windows of heaven and pour out for you a blessing until it overflows. Then I will rebuke the devourer for you, so that it will not destroy the fruits of the ground; nor will your vine in the field cast its grapes," says the LORD of hosts.
>
> "All the nations will call you blessed, for you shall be a delightful land," says the LORD of hosts.
>
> Malachi 3:10–12

The Scriptures are loaded with promises. When you read a promise, ask the Holy Spirit how you can sow into it. Once a young woman I was mentoring was struggling with financial lack. I taught her about the power of sowing with intentionality into the promise. I showed her one Scripture promise: "Give, and it will be given to you. They will pour into your lap a good measure—pressed down, shaken together, and running over. For by your standard of measure it will be measured to you in return" (Luke 6:38).

I explained to her that this promise is true, but that she needed to activate it. I challenged her to sow into it with intentionality. I instructed her to keep a little book in her handbag and every time she gave to someone (it could be buying a cup of coffee, helping someone with a task, giving some finances in an offering or to someone in need, or serving in some way), she was to write the date in her little book and the description of what she had sowed. She followed my instruction, and every time she wrote in her book, she thanked the Lord for the fulfillment of the promise in Luke 6:38. When she received blessings, she wrote that in her book too with a cross-reference to the seed sowed. Several months later she shared with me about the amazing breakthroughs she had. She was reaping a harvest from every seed she sowed. She had accessed the riches of heaven.

One time I was behind schedule and cried out to the Lord, "I do not have time to finish this!"

He replied, "You have more than enough time, because all the time you sow daily in My presence through your worship, prayers and service is collecting increase in heaven. Reap some time by faith right now." I did exactly that and before I knew it I not only had time to complete the project but time to spare. I now regularly reap time.

Realm #2: Blessing

In Genesis 26:12 we read about how Isaac sowed in difficult ground and reaped a hundredfold in that same year, but there was more. The Scripture states, "and the Lord blessed him." It is still true. In Christ, we are granted by His grace a realm of blessing. As defined previously, a realm is a domain, and God created you to live in the domain of His blessings. In Genesis 1:28 God made a declaration of blessing over all people: "God blessed them." You were never created for curse. Blessing is your portion when you are in Christ.

Isaac accessed this realm of blessing through sowing his seed. The Lord blessed him in addition to the hundredfold harvest from his seed. Often, when I sow a seed in one area of my life, I get blessed in other areas that I did not intentionally sow into. Sowing sets you up to move into the realm of blessing.

Jesus created a realm of perpetual abundance and goodness for you through His finished work on the cross. This realm has your name on it. You were created for blessing and blessed you shall be—He has promised. You can live in all the blessings of His goodness, health, victory, peace, joy, and prosperity all the days of your life in the earth.

When you live in this realm, you are blessed in everything you put your hands to. Your health is blessed. Your finances are blessed. Your family is blessed. Your workplace is blessed. Your relationships are blessed. Difficulties and challenges turn into blessings for you and curses flee from you when you live in the realm of blessing.

Many believers understand that when they finish their course of life in the earth, they will step into heaven where all is bliss. This is true, of course, but most do not understand that they can experience this realm now. Remember, "On earth as it is in heaven."

Deuteronomy 28:2 states, "All these blessings will come upon you and overtake you." You have probably seen football games when a player is aggressively tackled from behind and brought down to the ground under a pile of heavyweight athletes—he was "overtaken." Imagine what it would be like if blessings came upon your life in that way. They can and they will be attracted to you like metal to a magnet when you are established in the realm of blessing.

In Deuteronomy 28:1 we discover the qualifying terms for living in this realm: "*If* you diligently obey . . . *all* His commandments" (emphasis added). Whoops! What do we do now? How can we qualify? We have definitely not fulfilled that requirement. No one has obeyed *all* the Lord's commandments all the time . . . except for Jesus. And that is the point—*Jesus* did and always will. He fulfilled all the requirements for you, He made the way for you to live within all of God's promises, all the time. All the blessings revealed in the Bible are yours not because of your own righteousness but because of His. These heavenly riches do not belong to you because you are worthy, but because *He* is.

He fulfilled the requirements and gave you the blessings—blessings that will come upon you and overtake you on a perpetual basis. This is a great picture of what it means to live in the realm of blessing.

I remember one time ministering in Southeast Asia and Oceania. In our first city, my assistant and I were so blessed that we had to buy an extra suitcase to hold all the gifts we had been given. When we arrived at the airport, the check-in attendant weighed our bags and informed us that we would need to pay the equivalent of $900 in overweight charges. This was on an international flight. We were on our way to another nation where we would be flying on five domestic flights within a three-week period. The baggage allotment on domestic flights is even less, so I quickly calculated the overweight fees for all the flights that were still ahead of us.

Blessings had overtaken us for sure! Instead of paying the fees, we opened up the suitcase and gave away many of the gifts to people in the terminal. They were so happy as we blessed them in Jesus' name, and we were blessed to be a blessing!

When you live in God's realm of blessing, everything works together for good, and you will be blessed in everything you put your hands to. You will be blessed as you rise up in the morning and blessed when you sleep at night. All your relationships will be blessed. Your finances will be blessed. Your health will be blessed. You will increase in houses, lands, vehicles. You will be fruitful and multiply. You will be blessed with great favor. You will shine as a light in the darkest of places. Your righteousness will shine like the noonday (see Isaiah 58:10). Goodness and mercy shall follow you all the days of your life (see Psalm 23:6).

Realm #3: Rich

Isaac reaped and was blessed, but the Scripture also states that he became rich. Being rich is different from being blessed. For example, if I were to give you $1,000, you would be blessed, but that does not make you rich. "Rich" is a realm that is sustained. When you are rich, your sustained personal realm of abundance goes beyond merely possessing what you need. When you are rich, there is an overflow.

While in Egypt, Israel lived in a state of "not enough." Then they lived in the wilderness and lived in the state of "just enough." But when they entered the Promised Land, they lived in the state of "more than enough." The state of more than enough is that realm of "rich." But there is more; Scripture reveals that Isaac "continued to grow richer." God is a God of increase. He wants you to be fruitful and multiply. There is always more to receive from His glory.

Being rich in the Kingdom is not about how much money you have in the bank—although most people equate being rich with money and material goods. The world's economy is very fickle, and we should never put our trust in it. But when you are Kingdom-rich, you will have all the money you need and all the possessions you need in abundance. They follow you as you seek the Lord because the heavens are open over you. When you live in the state of "rich," you are content and there is no lack—only abundance. I have been rich for a long time. I am fully satisfied. I do not compare myself with the billionaires of the world because that is not how I gauge "rich." I have an abundance of all things. I am rich and continue to grow richer. You can too.

Our family lived in Mexico for a few years on a mission assignment. My husband and I and our two children lived in one small bedroom of a two-bedroom apartment shared with others. We built a bed out of plywood with a privacy board at the end and the boys' bunk beds on the other side of it. All the possessions we had in Mexico were kept with us in that room. In the other bedroom were three young men in bunk beds and we all shared one bathroom, a small kitchen and living area. We were as happy as could be. At that time in our lives, we did not have much money in the bank and our monthly income was minimal—yet we were so rich. We were comfortable and happy; we ate meals every day, had the transportation we needed, enjoyed great friendships, and saw people saved, healed and delivered daily. There was not a day when we lacked anything. We were full to the brim and probably much more fulfilled than most billionaires. We were rich!

Too often, people will seek after the world's goods, thinking that if they only had more money or possessions or vacations, they would be happier. Yet they often discover that the more they have, the more dissatisfied they become, always wanting more in order to feel fulfilled. As I have stated before, there is nothing wrong with having many material possessions. But they should not be your focus. If, instead of seeking them out, you seek the Kingdom, they will find you.

When you tap into the realm of heavenly riches, the material blessings will be added to you.

The Rich Young Ruler

We can learn some keen insights from the story of the rich young ruler:

> And someone came to Him and said, "Teacher, what good thing shall I do that I may obtain eternal life?"
>
> And He said to him, "Why are you asking Me about what is good? There is only One who is good; but if you wish to enter into life, keep the commandments."
>
> Then he said to Him, "Which ones?"
>
> And Jesus said, "You shall not commit murder; you shall not commit adultery; you shall not steal; you shall not bear false witness; honor your father and mother"; and "You shall love your neighbor as yourself."
>
> The young man said to Him, "All these things I have kept; what am I still lacking?"
>
> Jesus said to him, "If you wish to be complete, go and sell your possessions and give to the poor, and you will have treasure in heaven; and come, follow Me." But when the young man heard this statement, he went away grieving; for he was one who owned much property.
>
> And Jesus said to His disciples, "Truly I say to you, it is hard for a rich man to enter the kingdom of heaven. Again I say to you, it is easier for a camel to go through the eye of a needle, than for a rich man to enter the kingdom of God."
>
> Matthew 19:16–24

This young man, who was righteous in his conduct, wanted to obtain eternal life. After he asked Jesus, "What good thing shall I do that I may obtain eternal life?" Jesus' response was interesting, as He mentioned obedience to the law. I believe Jesus desired to reveal to this self-righteous young man that his own good works could not give him eternal life because if you live by the law, you have to obey *all* the law *all* the time. The young man proudly mentioned that he had kept all the commandments from his youth and he inquired to find out what else was required in order to enter the Kingdom.

Jesus' answer was for him to sell all his possessions and give to the poor, so that he would have treasure in heaven. Jesus did not ask the rich young ruler to give away his possessions in order to be poor but so that he would have treasure in heaven. What you sow on the earth gains interest and increase in heaven because there is a correlation between what you sow on the earth and your treasure in heaven.

When the young man heard this statement, he went away grieving because he owned much property. He was not ready to give up any of his riches in order to sow them. As Jesus explained to His disciples, it is hard for the rich to enter the Kingdom because their love for the riches can stand in the way.

So the rich young ruler left poor in spirit and without the ability to access heaven's treasure. He was too wrapped up in his worldly possessions to grasp the idea that our possessions do not grant us true riches. He could not comprehend that the true treasure is *Jesus*, and that when we make Him the center of our lives, *He* becomes the focus of our passions and our desires. Then natural riches follow from heaven.

That is what happened in the case of Isaac; he followed God's instructions by faith and became rich, and then, the Scripture says, he became even richer. Once you own a realm of rich, it can increase.

Realm #4: Wealth

The fourth realm that Isaac entered through his sowing was the realm of wealth. The Scripture explains that in addition to reaping a hundredfold, being blessed, becoming rich and richer, he also became "extremely wealthy." Wealth is different from rich. Being rich is about your personal abundance, but wealth is how you influence the world with what you have been enriched with.

I am extremely wealthy. Again, this is not based on how much money I have in the bank or how many material possessions I have (although I am blessed in these things), it is based on the way I have influenced the world with the riches I have been entrusted with.

Every day, I am able to sow the Word into the world through my preaching and media ministry, I am mentoring people in the things of God. I am reaching the lost, caring for widows and orphans, and giving finances and material provision. All the riches of the gifts and resource God has given me are influencing the world for His glory, and all of that creates eternal reward, too. Oh, I love being wealthy! God wants to bless all His people with wealth.

Perhaps you are already wealthy, but you have not realized it. If you embrace the standards of the world you will be blinded to the reality of the true wealth you may already have obtained.

Wealthy King Solomon

I love the story in the Bible where the heathen Queen of Sheba visited King Solomon (see 1 Kings 10). King Solomon was living in the blessing realm of God beyond any other in the areas of wisdom and wealth.

The queen found it next to impossible to believe the reports she had been told regarding Solomon's wisdom and wealth. Hence, she decided to pay a visit to Solomon and tested him with difficult questions. He was able to answer every one with the magnificent wisdom that God had granted him. Solomon then escorted her on a tour of his estate. She was so overwhelmed with the wealth of Solomon's house that "there was no more spirit in her" (verse 5)—it took her breath away.

This is a picture of the abundance God is calling you to. God wants you to amaze those who do not know Him. When they see God's goodness in your life, they will be drawn to Him—this is exactly what happened to the Queen of Sheba. She was attracted to God, and after beholding all of Solomon's wealth, she said,

> "Behold, the half was not told me. You exceed in wisdom and prosperity the report which I heard. How blessed are your men, how blessed are these your servants who stand before you continually and hear your wisdom. Blessed be the Lord your God who delighted in you to set you on the throne of Israel; because the Lord loved Israel forever, therefore He made you king, to do justice and righteousness."
>
> 1 Kings 10:7–9

You, like Solomon, are invited to live in the glory of your God's wealth as His king and priest: "[He] hath made us kings and priests unto God and his Father; to him be glory and dominion for ever and ever. Amen" (Revelation 1:6 KJV). It is all yours.

Jesus said, "Fear not, little flock; for it is your Father's good pleasure to give you the kingdom" (Luke 12:32 KJV).

The glory the Father gave Jesus has been given to you (see John 17:22). Isaiah 60:1–10 foresees that there will be a people who arise in the light of Jesus Christ who will manifest a level of glory that will literally attract the attention of kings and nations—and their wealth. You, like Solomon, can cause the nations to be drawn to the brightness of your rising.

Like Solomon, you are God's "king" in the earth, set in place to manifest His wealth. You, like Solomon, can ask for wisdom and it will be granted generously and without reproach: "If any of you lacks wisdom, let him ask of God, who gives to all generously and without reproach, and it will be given to him" (James 1:5).

Wealth attracts more wealth. The Queen of Sheba brought many blessings to Solomon. Solomon did not need any more camels, gold, spices or timber, but because he lived in the realm of wealth, more was added to him.

Wealth = Influence

Whoever holds the greatest wealth in the world will potentially have the greatest influence in the world—for good or for evil. So many corrupt individuals are obtaining great wealth through things like sex, slave labor, drugs, weapons and organ trafficking. This evil realm of wealth needs to be overthrown by those who steward righteous wealth.

Every believer should desire to live in the realm of wealth in order to give glory to God and to overthrow the works of the wicked. We carry stronger authority in the world when we are wealthy. That is why we should position ourselves to live in the realm of "extreme wealth." God did it for Isaac and for Solomon—He can do it for you.

In the next chapter, I will teach you some special keys for how to create your realm of abundance. When you learn the principles of contending for a realm, breakthrough will accelerate, and you will enjoy living in the atmosphere of heavenly riches.

SUMMARY

Genesis 26:12–13 reveals four realms of abundance that God desires to bless all His people with:

1. **Realm #1 Reaping the harvest that you have sown.** "Now Isaac sowed in that land and reaped." Just as a farmer does, we must always sow with intentionality and expectation and then harvest purposefully. We can sow and reap finances, time, relationships and the Word (i.e., decreeing His promises).
2. **Realm #2 Blessing.** "And the Lord blessed him." Sowing seed sets you up to move into the realm of blessing. Jesus created a realm of perpetual abundance and goodness for you through His finished work on the cross. You can live in all the blessings of His goodness, health, victory, peace, joy and prosperity all the days of your life in the earth.
3. **Realm #3 Rich.** "And the man became rich." "Rich" is a sustained personal realm of abundance, beyond necessities. When you are rich, there is an overflow. When you are "Kingdom-rich" you will have money and possessions in abundance. They follow you as you seek the Lord because the heavens are opened over you.

4. **Realm #4 Wealth.** "He became very wealthy. " While being rich is about your personal abundance, having wealth is about your influence on the world with what your life has been enriched with. When others observe that God's goodness is apparent in your life, they will be drawn to Him, as the Queen of Sheba was attracted to God after beholding Solomon's wealth. It is your portion to live in the realm of "extreme wealth."

QUESTIONS TO PONDER

1. Which of these four realms are you experiencing at this point? How do you know?
2. It all begins with sowing. What are you sowing right now, and what is the harvest you are contending for? How has sowing in the past brought you to where you are now?
3. What is keeping you from stepping into the next level? Examine your life; could it be that you are already there but have not recognized it?

MAKE THIS DECLARATION OVER YOUR LIFE

I thank You because You came so that I may have abundant life. I am a faithful, intentional steward, always sowing in good soil so that I reap an abundant harvest that is more than enough. Everything that pertains to me and that I put my hand to is blessed. Indeed, I am beyond blessed—for I am Kingdom-rich. I live in abundance with overflow, so much that with my wealth I am able to impact others for God.

5

Creating Realms of Abundance

> And God said, Let there be . . .
>
> Genesis 1:3 KJV

The Lord called my husband and me to leave our careers in 1980 and serve Him full time on the mission field. Moreover I was to serve in pulpit ministry, equipping believers. When He offered us the invitation, He added that He would teach us to live by faith with no visible means of support. We were not to share our needs with anyone but Him. We were excited about this opportunity, having heard amazing missionary testimonies regarding supernatural support and provision. We had searched the Scriptures from Genesis to Revelation and were sure of God's promises to provide well for those who believed in faith. I was fully convinced that it was going to be a blissfully glorious faith journey. But it was not—at least it sure did not feel like that.

In fact, I was fairly sure that the devil had our name highlighted for assault by every spirit of lack and poverty in the universe. Every day we seemed to face harsh resistance to the life of "God-abundance."

We had written out the scriptural promises pertaining to God's provision and we stood on them by making decrees regularly. Obeying everything taught in the Word regarding Kingdom economy, we had no Plan B. We had made a complete commitment to abandon all and follow God by faith. There was no turning back.

Some days began with no food in the house—not just no food that we liked, but *no food*. We once enjoyed a "faith meal"—we sat with empty plates believing there was food on them. At times, I would open the fridge and find it absolutely empty, but I would proceed to confess out loud that God's provision was there. The Scripture teaches us to call those things that are not as though they are (see Romans 4:17), and I had lots of practice doing that—not only for food but also for gasoline for the car, clothing and school supplies for the children and other daily needs.

To the glory of God, even though we started some days with no food, we never went to bed without having anything to eat that day and I was always able to get to where I needed to be (albeit sometimes through very creative ways). God was with us, but we had to fight for every inch of ground we took in the spirit. Not only did we have to fight against the daunting circumstances but also discouragement, self-condemnation, shame and doubt. It was a very trying time.

After five years of tests and trials, things changed suddenly. I was driving down the road on my way to a ministry engagement, crying out to God. Suddenly, I felt a breakthrough in my spirit. I had an immediate "knowing" deep inside that our warfare had ended. Within two weeks of that day, victory began to become manifest in every area of our lives. Divine provision flooded in.

Following this sudden breakthrough, God called us to Tijuana, Mexico, where at the time close to 80 percent of the population lived in dire poverty. Through our earlier persistence, we had gained authority over poverty and were able to care for the poor in Mexico without hindrance. Once you contend against doubt and unbelief for the promises of God, you gain authority in that realm.

In Tijuana, we built houses for the poor, fed and clothed those in the slums and built medical clinics and orphanages. We cared for the fatherless, widows, and those in prison and taught people how to be free from lack. It was a glorious season and we were fruitful in every endeavor. We had gained the realm! The heavens were open and the enemy was under our feet. We enjoyed the overflow!

Since that time we have successfully ministered to the poor and destitute in many nations. When you contend for the realm, you win the realm. You gain access to the riches of heaven in that area of your life.

In other words, once you prevail through a trial, you win operative authority in that area of testing. Having pressed through to victory, we gained authority in the realm of material blessings and financial provision. The heavens were opened over us, and they still are!

Tests are not pleasant but when you endure, you gain spiritual maturity as well as abundance. That is why James wrote:

> Consider it all joy, my brethren, when you encounter various trials, knowing that the testing of your faith produces

> endurance. And let endurance have its perfect result, so that you may be perfect and complete, lacking in nothing.
>
> James 1:2–4[1]

Contending for Your Realm

As defined previously, a realm is a domain, or a place where you have authority. Many people fail to secure a realm of blessing in God because they do not press in; they become discouraged when they face resistance.

I find the story of Elisha and King Joash interesting (see 2 Kings 13:14–19). Joash needed breakthrough from his enemies (Aram), and he obeyed what Elisha told him to do. He failed, however, to persevere in striking the ground until the breakthrough came. He struck the ground only three times instead of continuing until the victory was secured. Here is the story:

> When Elisha became sick with the illness of which he was to die, Joash the king of Israel came down to him and wept over him and said, "My father, my father, the chariots of Israel and its horsemen!"
>
> Elisha said to him, "Take a bow and arrows." So he took a bow and arrows. Then he said to the king of Israel, "Put your hand on the bow." And he put his hand on it, then Elisha laid his hands on the king's hands. He said, "Open the window toward the east," and he opened it. Then Elisha said, "Shoot!" And he shot. And he said, "The LORD's arrow of victory, even the arrow of victory over Aram; for you will defeat the Arameans at Aphek until you have destroyed them."
>
> Then he said, "Take the arrows," and he took them. And he said to the king of Israel, "Strike the ground," and he

> struck it three times and stopped. So the man of God was angry with him and said, "You should have struck five or six times, then you would have struck Aram until you would have destroyed it. But now you shall strike Aram only three times."
>
> 2 Kings 13:14–19

The lesson: Never leave a battle unfinished. You gain your victory only when you stand strong until the end.

The apostle Paul also urges us to stand firm until the end. He identifies the spiritual battle that is behind the assaults we face and he exhorts us to stand unwavering in Christ and His authority.

> Finally, be strong in the Lord and in the strength of His might. Put on the full armor of God, so that you will be able to stand firm against the schemes of the devil. For our struggle is not against flesh and blood, but against the rulers, against the powers, against the world forces of this darkness, against the spiritual forces of wickedness in the heavenly places.
>
> Therefore, take up the full armor of God, so that you will be able to resist in the evil day, and having done everything, to stand firm.
>
> Ephesians 6:10–13

God's Word says, "Believe in the Lord Jesus and you shall be saved, you *and your household*" (Acts 16:31, emphasis added). We know it is God's will for all to be saved, and He promises that if we pray according to His will, He hears us and if we know that He hears us, then we can have full assurance about receiving the answer to our prayer (see 1 John 5:14–15[2]). God's will for all to know Him is also confirmed in

Psalm 2:8 (KJV): "Ask of me and I shall give thee the heathen for thine inheritance." Are you a believer? Believers have been promised household salvations.

I met a woman at a conference resource table who asked for prayer for her daughter. She explained that her daughter, Ginger, had grown up in the Lord, but her boyfriend introduced her to drugs when she was in her late teens and she immediately became addicted. At that point, Ginger had been addicted for thirteen years to cocaine and had been in and out of jails and prisons. She had given birth to three daughters, and all had been removed from her care as she was deemed unfit to raise them.

The mother prayed for her daughter daily, but year after year Ginger's condition got worse instead of better. She had obtained a book of Scripture decrees, and I encouraged her to decree the Word over her daughter every day. The Word does not return void; it goes forth in the realm of the spirit and accomplishes everything it is sent to do (see Isaiah 55:10–11[3]).

Almost two years later I saw this faithful mother again. She reported no improvement in her daughter when she first began decreeing the Word. In fact, Ginger continued to spiral downward. But she never gave up. She continued to decree the Word in faith. She kept "striking the ground" until breakthrough came. Just the week before we connected, Ginger had come to her mother, desperate to leave her hellish life behind. For the first time in fifteen years, her daughter had showed a genuine interest in changing.

At the time, we hosted a restoration program for people coming off the streets and out of prison, and Ginger was accepted into it. God miraculously delivered her from the addiction without tormenting withdrawal—it was supernatural.

One day just over three weeks into her time with us, I noticed her writing furiously on a tablet in the corner. She radiated the glory of God. I inquired, "Hey, what's happening?"

She replied, "God is downloading a book to me on how to walk out of addiction." (The book, *Walk It Out*, is now published and has been distributed into many prisons all over the United States.)

When Ginger finished the program, she came on staff with us in our resource department and later became its manager. Opportunities came for her to share her testimony. God restored her relationship with her daughters. It was amazing. Talk about the riches of heaven!

Ginger's dream was to marry a man of God and to have a child that she could raise, having missed that with her daughters. The Lord answered the prayer gloriously. The husband God gave her is definitely from the treasury in heaven, and she gave birth to twins: a boy and a girl! Ginger eventually served in our missions department and was also able to start her own ministry.

Ginger's mother had created a realm of victory for her daughter's life. She contended for breakthrough until she obtained it. She never gave up. Now God is using her to impart faith, encouragement and breakthrough to others.

Notice that Ginger's victory did not become manifest the moment her mother began praying. It took many years, but every prayer, every tear and every decree was collected in the heavens where they kept gaining equity.

Have you been standing in faith for years without a victorious outcome? Have confidence that your faith is being honored. Keep striking the ground.

A friend of mine suffered a serious injury in an accident that required surgery. The surgery was botched. As a result, she suffered excruciating pain for twenty-seven years. She could not walk without a walker or assistance, and she had to take large doses of morphine to help manage the pain. Throughout, she stood in faith, believing for her healing, never losing sight of the promises of God, always confessing her healing.

One Sunday while she and her husband were on vacation, they visited a church. A woman who was part of the church's ministry team prayed at the altar for her, and that is where her healing began. Over the next three days, all the pain lifted. She was completely pain-free. Her body, however, continued to be dependent upon the morphine. She believed the Lord told her to come off the morphine "cold turkey." Even though she suffered some withdrawal symptoms, the grace of God was with her and she was completely delivered of the need for this narcotic in less than a week.

Her years of standing in faith produced a realm of victory for her. Not only did she experience her own healing, but now she encourages many others. She shares her testimony with so much authority that many others receive encouragement and faith for their own healings.

I do not understand why some breakthroughs take so long to manifest themselves. Most battles are not as grueling as these, but they illustrate the importance of standing on the Word in the midst of your battle, large or small. Blessing and victory result from such persistent faith.

Do you see how it works? Whenever you win a battle, you earn authority in that realm. Operative authority gets established when you resist and persist long enough to see a breakthrough.

Your breakthrough begins when you receive insight and revelation from God. If you are facing some difficulty right now, seek the Lord for His promises concerning a victorious outcome. What does His Word say? If God says it, you can believe it, and that settles it! Never let your circumstances define you or move you—stand firm on the Word of God. When the Spirit of God quickens a Word to you, it is your invitation to receive it as your very own personal promise—and to build a realm with it.

Your season of resistance may not be short. God does not always take you out of the battle, but He will always walk you through it. Some believers I know have battled for over twenty years before their breakthrough. It is true: The greater the battle, the greater the victory and testimony.

Our ministry once went through a ferocious three-and-a-half-year-long spiritual assault. It hit every area of my life and ministry: confidence, health, finance, relationships, favor, emotions and awareness of God's presence. The warfare at times was crushing—I had never in my many previous years of life with God faced anything like it. The enemy was assaulting the core of my spirituality: my faith and my love. If he could successfully assault my faith, he could destroy my ministry and calling. If he could successfully assault my love, he could destroy my message. The more I stood on the Word, the more intense the battle. The more I sowed financially, the more I was attacked in that area.

I continued to stand on the Word, embracing the truth and denying the enemy access to my realm. To be honest, though, I was definitely not Faith Woman every moment in the battle. There were hours when deep discouragement brought me into emotional despair and I lost sight of the promises, but

God always helped me regain focus. He is faithful. In all the places where we fail, His blood is enough. He literally erases the very existence of our failures when we humble ourselves, confess our sins and receive his forgiveness and cleansing: "If we confess our sins, He is faithful and righteous to forgive us our sins and to cleanse us from all unrighteousness" (1 John 1:9).

When the battle was finally won, a whole new realm of operative authority opened up and expanded our outreach; instead of my faith and love being weakened, they were greatly strengthened.

When you are creating a realm, you must endure the tests. God will be with you even when you do not feel Him. He is right beside you every step of the way.

The following is a review of how to build a realm:

1. **Receive the promises.** Take personal ownership of the promises of God that pertain to your situation. Meditate on the promises and stand on the Word of victory.
2. **Declare the breakthrough.** Out of the abundance of your heart, your mouth will speak and your words are powerful. Declare your breakthrough. Declare the Word with determination to carve out a realm of victory and testimony.
3. **Sow into the promise.** Isaac received the word of the Lord to live in Gerar. As Isaac sowed into the land, he carved out all four realms of abundance. Ginger's mother sowed prayers and decrees. My husband and I sowed prayers, decrees, finances and material possessions. Ask the Lord what seed to sow.

4. **Pass the test of your faith during seasons of resistance.** Stand on the Word in faith against all obstacles that resist you. Stand firm against the enemy's spiritual and circumstantial assaults. Do not waiver in unbelief. When you stand strong and persevere, you will gain authority.

Stewarding Your Realm

Many believers, including ministers, have lost their hard-won realm because they failed to steward it well. One surprising example in Scripture is Solomon. As we noted earlier, Solomon had sought the Lord for wisdom, and God had given him a realm of great wealth. However, he fell into idolatry and immorality, and his blessings diminished at the end of his life.

When believers rise and then fall, the two most predominant factors I have noticed that contribute to the loss of their realms are: (1) sin, and (2) discouragement that contributes to loss of faith.

One leader I knew and very much admired contended for a realm of supernatural healing, miracles and revival. He stood on God's Word and spent hours in the presence of God praying, travailing and soaking in heavenly glory. As a result, people began to receive healing and miracles, and the realm grew until he had a massive global influence. Multitudes of people came to Christ and were touched by the supernatural blessing of God. He knew how to access heavenly riches and every area of his ministry was blessed. His ministry was an authentic display of God's grace, revelation and power. Unfortunately, he fell into some significant sin and he lost the realm. Even though he was personally restored on many levels and he stepped back into ministry, it was never the same.

Joshua and Caleb had lived in the wilderness the same as others but they did not allow discouragement to settle in their hearts—they nurtured their faith. When they went in to spy out the Promised Land, they came back with a good report while the others came back discouraged, having seen the giants and becoming convinced that they could never conquer them. God had promised them a land flowing with milk and honey, but the discouragement of the other men stripped them of their faith. As a result, they did not enter into the Promised Land, while Joshua and Caleb did.

Stewardship is important when you are handling heavenly riches. Jesus said, "Everyone to whom much is given, from him much will be required" (Luke 12:48 NKJV). God firmly reminded Israel when they were going into the Promised Land that He was the source of all their blessing and the one who gave them the power to make wealth. If they disobeyed Him or went after other gods, they would perish (see Deuteronomy 8). Paul also warned believers about disqualification (see 2 Corinthians 13:5; 1 Corinthians 9:27).

Another aspect of stewardship is God's expectation for you to bring increase from what He has given you. My husband and I carved out a realm of faith for the provision of God to come into our lives, but that realm has grown over the years as we have believed God for more levels of provision to accomplish His mandates. We continue to honor Him with the first of all the increase. In the future, our faith should be producing more fruit than it is now.

Remember the conclusion of Jesus' parable about stewardship?

> And he said to him, "Out of your own mouth I will judge you, you wicked servant. You knew that I was an austere man, collecting what I did not deposit and reaping what I did not sow. Why then did you not put my money in the bank, that at my coming I might have collected it with interest?" And he said to those who stood by, "Take the mina from him, and give it to him who has ten minas."
>
> (But they said to him, "Master, he has ten minas.")
>
> For I say to you, that to everyone who has will be given; and from him who does not have, even what he has will be taken away from him.
>
> Luke 19:22–26 NKJV

Jesus' parable was about a nobleman who went on a trip, leaving each of his ten servants with the same amount of money, which he expected them to do business with. When he returned, he praised those who brought him increase on the original amount he had entrusted to them and he rewarded them with more. However, one servant simply returned the original amount without increase, explaining that he was afraid to do more than to keep it safe. His master was angry. Jesus' stated His point: "I tell you that to everyone who has, more shall be given, but from the one who does not have, even what he does have shall be taken away" (Luke 19:26).

When you have been granted access to the riches of heaven, God expects increase from what He gives you. Work the realm, establish the realm—and *increase*.

In the next chapter, you will learn to activate your faith in order to receive the riches of heaven that have been earmarked for you.

SUMMARY

1. **God has given us the power and authority to create realms of abundance.** However, this does not necessarily happen overnight. We must contend for it. Once we prevail, we will have operative authority in that realm.
2. **Follow four steps for building a realm:** (1) Take personal ownership of the promises of God that pertain to your situation, standing on the Word of victory. (2) Declare the breakthrough. Declare the Word with determination. (3) Sow into the promise. Sow prayers and decrees, finances and possessions. Ask the Lord what seed to sow, then sow. (4) Pass the testing of your faith. Stand on the Word in faith against all obstacles that resist you until you receive victory and the resulting authority.
3. **Steward your realm well.** Do not lose it through sin or discouragement. God expects you to bring increase from what He has given you. Work the realm, establish the realm—and increase.

QUESTIONS TO PONDER

1. Have you had to contend for realms of provision and abundance in your own life? What were (or are) some of the trials and resistance you have experienced? Have you achieved the victory or are you still "in process"?
2. What realm are you needing to build now? Look at the four steps to building a realm. What have you done, or are doing, in each area to build this realm? Do you have a plan of action?

3. How are you stewarding the realm that is already yours? Are there any areas of discouragement or temptation that you need to deal with in order to not lose it? What are you doing to bring increase?

MAKE THIS DECLARATION OVER YOUR LIFE

God has given me the power and authority to create realms of abundance. I diligently and faithfully contend for the realm of ______________, standing on the promises God has given me for this situation. His Word is always true, so I take ownership of these promises and the breakthrough that comes with them. I will not allow obstacles, setbacks, doubts, discouragement or anything else to hinder me. I will press on, listening to the Lord and obeying His leading at all times. The victory is mine.

6

Accessing the Riches of Heaven by Faith

> Now faith is the substance of things hoped for, the evidence of things not seen.
>
> Hebrews 11:1 NKJV

I was only a few weeks old in the Lord when I noticed an employment opportunity in the local newspaper. My husband and I were building a second home at the time and needed the extra income to cover the extra payments. He worked the afternoon shift, so I was looking for a full-time day shift, which would allow one of us to always be with our children, both of whom were under two years old.

I had a medical background in nursing, but I had never worked in a lab. The job I applied for was in a medical lab where I would only need to draw blood and do some reception work. I felt confident that I could accomplish the necessary tasks. It was less money than I would make as a nurse on call but the daytime hours with weekends off were consistent, which was perfect.

When I went in person to present my résumé, I discovered that a hundred and thirty candidates had already applied, and that many of them had previous lab experience. But I was not discouraged as I had just finished reading a faith-building book titled, *How to Live Like a King's Kid*, which had assured me that all things were possible in God. I left the office with faith-filled confidence that I would have favor and be hired for the position.

The following Monday I received a call that I was on the short list of twenty. I was delighted—until they explained to me that one of the qualifications for the position was that I had to be capable of typing a minimum of 45 words a minute with accuracy. They scheduled me for a typing test three days later. I had failed typing in school and I had never learned (to this day) to type without looking at the keys. The best I had ever typed was eighteen to twenty words per minute. After that shocking news, I regained my composure and stirred my faith to believe I would pass the test. I only had three days to practice my typing. But I was a "King's Kid" and believed I could do all things through Christ who strengthened me!

I borrowed a typewriter, prayed and began to practice. I called on God with unwavering faith to help me as I typed hour after hour. Yet by the time I was to take the test, the highest score I had ever reached in my practice sessions was 28 words per minute—far from the 45-words-per-minute goal.

Nevertheless, the morning of my typing test I left the house full of faith, thinking, *It really does not matter what I can or cannot do in the natural. God, You are a supernatural God, so You can give me supernatural typing skills because I am a King's Kid and all things are possible in You*. God would get all the glory as I had no natural ability.

I arrived for the typing test and waited in the reception lobby until they called my name. I kept thinking: *All things are possible in God. He will empower me to type 45 words per minute with accuracy.* Finally, my name was called. They seated me at a typewriter, but to my horror, it was an electric one. I had never used an electric typewriter before. (Yes, this was way back when electric typewriters were new, before computers.) I did not even know how to turn on the typewriter. They showed me how it worked. Through my fear I pressed on, repeating to myself *I can do all things through Christ who strengthens me*. They gave me five minutes to practice, but the practice session produced more horror—I was a "lead foot" on the keys and one touch on a key would print a letter ten to fifteen times.

It was finally time for them to start the clock. My only hope was to believe God. In the natural, I would fail the test for sure. Intentionally, I believed with all my heart that God would cause me to triumph.

I typed away until the bell rang. The woman who was testing me asked me to go back out into the reception area and wait for the results. A few minutes later, she came and reported, "You passed the test at 48 words per minute." Yay, God!

The following week, I was invited for another interview. This time there were only three of us on the short list. The other two had many years of experience in medical laboratory work, and I was the least experienced. I was unmoved, believing that I was a King's Kid and highly favored by God with undeserved, unmerited favor. The next day, I received the call—I had been awarded the position!

This job turned out to be way beyond what I expected. It worked perfectly for our financial and schedule needs, yet the greatest blessing was that mature Christians made up over 70 percent of the staff. Every day at work they discipled me as a new believer. We studied the Bible during our breaks; held prayer meetings and enjoyed fellowship times. I could ask all the questions I wanted.

In addition, I had favor with three of the non-Christian girls on the staff and I was able to lead two of them to the Lord, sowing valuable "love-seeds" into the other.

You see, all things are possible when you believe, and God will do "exceedingly abundantly above all that we ask or think" (Ephesians 3:20 NKJV).

Faith—Your Heavenly Currency

Faith pleases God. In fact, Hebrews 11:6 states that without faith you cannot please Him. As mentioned in a previous chapter, God has already given us every spiritual blessing in the heavenly places (see Ephesians 1:3) *and* everything that pertains to life and godliness (see 2 Peter 1:3). Faith is the heavenly currency with which to make exchanges in God's heavenly dimension. All the promises that Jesus purchased on Calvary are in your "heavenly bank account," filled to the brim. When you connect with faith to the promises of God, you have the ability to make withdrawals from that account.

Your Most Holy Faith

The Bible says that everyone has a measure of faith (see Romans 12:3). This is what enables people to believe. Even unsaved people have the ability to believe. After all, God created humans in His image and because He has the ability to believe, people do too. There is a faith, however, that only believers in Christ possess—it is a "most holy faith" (Jude 1:20). This is the same faith that Jesus operated in when He raised the dead, healed the sick, cast out devils, cleansed the lepers and worked miracles. His faith resides in your spirit when you are born again. You have access to His faith.

Mark 11:22 says, "Have faith in God." Many Bible scholars believe that this Scripture can more accurately be translated "have God's faith" or "have God-like faith."[1] Jesus taught that this is the kind of faith that moves mountains and He explained how it works in verse 24: "Whatever things you ask when you pray, believe that you receive them, and you will have them"(NKJV).

It is this kind of "God-faith" that connects you to the riches of heaven. This faith grows in you by allowing the Spirit of God to quicken His eternal truth to you.

Have you ever read a familiar verse in Scripture and suddenly it is as if the words jump off the page? It speaks directly to your heart in ways that it never did before. That "quickened word" is what births faith in your heart.

Romans 10:17 says, "Faith comes from hearing, and hearing by the word of Christ." The root Greek word for "word" in that passage is *rhema*, or the Spirit-infused and quickened word. When the Holy Spirit gives this type of revelation, it produces faith that enables you to take ownership of the promise. The promise then becomes your personal promise—your personal reality. Deuteronomy 29:29 confirms that "the secret things belong to the Lord our God, but the things revealed belong to us and to our sons forever."

Facts Are Temporal—Truth Is Eternal

Facts and truth are not the same thing. Facts are temporal and subject to change, but truth is eternal, forever settled in God. As believers, we live according to the truth of God's Word, not according to temporal facts. We can acknowledge facts, but only as facts, not the truth.

For example, someone who is very dear to me is battling a chronic, debilitating illness. The diagnosis of this illness is merely a fact, as are the symptoms. But the diagnosis and the symptoms are not the truth. The truth is that by the stripes of Jesus my loved one is healed (see 1 Peter 2:24)—he was healed by Christ's finished work on the cross two thousand years ago. Every day, the facts (symptoms) need to be attended to in order to bring comfort and encouragement to him, but facts are not an eternal reality; they are temporal and subject to change. I am not asking God to heal my loved one; he was already healed through Christ's finished work on the cross and my faith has accessed and received that blessing. I do not have to beg God and pray, "Oh God, Oh God, please heal him!" No way! Because Jesus said, "Whatever things you ask when you pray, believe that you receive them, and you will have them."

He did not say you will have your request when you can see the answer, but rather when you believe that you receive. Now we are simply waiting for the *manifestation* of his healing. At some point, the truth *will* manifest itself. Rather than constantly asking for the same thing over and over again, believe that you receive when you pray. When you connect with your God-faith, then eagerly await the manifestation. As you wait, praise the Lord for the manifestation of what you have asked. Praise Him throughout the journey and cultivate fresh expectation for the manifestation, refreshing your active faith.

At times, for reasons unknown to us, the healing or the answer to prayer manifests itself on the other side of time, but whether it manifests on this side of time or the other, it will surely manifest—and that is the truth! Our faith is grounded, activated and substantiated by unchanging eternal truth and not by temporal outward manifestations of the truth.

Hebrews 11 gives us a list of the "heroes of faith." These believed God concerning the Messiah. They never let their faith weaken, although they never saw the manifestation of the promise in their lifetime. "All these, having gained approval through their faith, did not receive what was promised" (Hebrews 11:39).

We know that the promise of the Messiah *did* become a fact. Those heroes of faith did not see the fulfillment of the promise until they had passed into eternity, but it did happen! Authentic faith is based on the eternal truth revealed in the Scriptures.

Heavenly Downloads

In our days of modern computer technology, we are able to "download" information from the cyber realm simply by clicking a button. The information then comes from the "cloud" to our computer. Amazing! In a way, this is a picture of how you can download the riches of God's promises from heaven. *Faith* is the button that triggers the download.

We need to remember three special features of faith: (1) Faith is in the *now*, (2) Faith is the substance of what you hope for, and (3) Faith is evidence: "*Now* faith is the *substance* of things hoped for, the *evidence* of things not seen" (Hebrews 11:1 NKJV, emphasis added).

When you are engaged in faith, it is a "now" reality. Hope is activated toward the future but faith is in the "now." Hope says, "I have many bills and no money to pay them at this time but God will make a way somehow." This is future expectation (hope), not of faith. A confession of faith would sound different, something like, "Thank You, Lord, that these bills are paid in full and my bank accounts are replenished." Faith is a "now" statement. With active faith, a confession like this one is not empty words. Faith connects to the reality of the truth now. Faith calls those things that are not as though they are (see Romans 4:17). In fact, the bills might still be piled high and there is no money in the bank, yet true faith from the Spirit of God will acknowledge the promise as already delivered.

This is possible because faith is the substance of what you hope for. Hope, a joyful expectation for a positive outcome, is valuable, but only as a springboard to faith.

As a new believer (and the only believer in my family), I was excited about all my family and extended family one day coming to know the Lord. I was hopeful and had a joyful expectation, but I was not yet in faith. One day while reading my Bible, the Holy Spirit quickened a Scripture to my heart: "Believe on the Lord Jesus Christ and you will be saved, you and your house" (Acts 16:31 NKJV). It was a powerful moment. Faith entered me. This was no longer print on a page but an internal reality. I "knew that I knew that I knew"—God had promised that all my family was His. I had moved from hope to true faith, and it was a "now" reality. It was *eternally* true, *internally* true, *absolutely* true. Even though none of my family members had personally accepted Christ yet, I knew that their salvation was already a reality. No matter what their behavior was like (and some were openly against Christianity), I knew by faith that they were in God's Kingdom. Unquestionably.

One by one they came into a personal confession of faith; it occurred over a span of many years. I never wavered in my vision for them because faith is the reality; the actual substance of what I hoped for.

Faith is the evidence, the proof. Evidence carries judicial weight because it is proof. The morning following the night I was born again, I visited a group of friends who were in a New Age community I belonged to. We were all seeking spiritual light but were grossly deceived. I was so excited to share with them that their search was over because I had discovered the truth in Jesus; that He could forgive their sins as He forgave mine. In my naïvety, I assumed that the only reason they had not yet received Jesus was that they had not heard.

They listened to everything I said, then vehemently argued, "How can you believe this garbage? How do you know Jesus is the only way? Who says we have sin? Why do you think Jesus is even real?"

It was not the response I was expecting, for sure. I was shocked at their reaction and struggled to answer. "Well, because, the Bible says so." (I had not actually read the Bible at that point, but I assumed it said that Jesus is Savior and that He forgives our sins.) They shot the next question at me in disdain: "What? The Bible? How can you trust the Bible? It was written by a bunch of people. Anyone can write a Bible!"

I had no answer for them through my intellect, but I found myself blurting out loudly with confidence, "I just *know*! My 'knower' knows." Their derision did not move me. My faith alone was unshakable evidence, living proof.

When the Holy Spirit reveals a promise to you, you can receive the faith to secure it. The promise becomes an internal reality within your heart regardless of the outward situation, and your faith will produce the manifestation of the riches of God's goodness.

Activating Your Faith

A number of years ago, I was hosting a large event that was the greatest step of faith we had taken financially as a ministry up to that time. As we initially sought the Lord to receive His direction for the conference, we felt confident to move forward even though our faith was stretched. The Lord had given us numerous promises from the Scriptures, and we had a strong inner peace to say "yes" to the assignment. The budget continued to swell as we received further guidance about adding more details, speakers and musicians, and my faith started to wobble. I sought the Lord in prayer and once again He confirmed His will by giving more Scripture promises in addition to three unsolicited prophetic words of confirmation from random sources. My faith was refreshed and strengthened as we moved forward. The event budget continued to increase due to a number of complications, but we remained steadfast in faith.

At the last service of the event, we were still one hundred thousand dollars short of making the budget. My husband and I had already committed to giving our home as an offering if needed in order to fulfill our commitments for the event, even though we had received promises from the Lord that provision would be there. Just the night before, one of my intercessors had come to me with a powerful vision she had received in prayer: "I saw the heavens open and money coming down into our midst, enough to make the budget." When she shared the vision, faith entered my heart. I knew with absolute confidence that the need was met. In the natural, it was next to impossible, as the same people had been in the meeting for five days and had already given more than generously toward the conference budget.

That night during worship, a group of young people began to throw money down onto the platform from the balcony above. The rest of the worship was filled with spontaneous giving by the conference participants. Money literally rained down upon the platform from the balconies (as in the vision) and people were coming from every direction with offerings. No one requested an offering. This spontaneous giving went on for a long time. When the conference was over, every expense had been met, with a little extra. We had accessed God's riches of heaven.

At a different event, a fellow minister needed a substantial offering on the last night to complete a conference budget. When his team counted the offering, it was short by a significant amount. They were momentarily discouraged until they received a word from the Lord. The Spirit said, "Count it again." Excitement rose in their hearts and they recounted.

(When the Spirit speaks to you, obey quickly because sometimes the faith for the miracle is within the immediate response.) This time there was a significant increase to their initial total. They were happily surprised. The Spirit said, "Count it again." They recounted and it increased again. They recounted several times until the final need was met. Their faith had tapped into the miracle realm.

When you access a Spirit-quickened word, you have access to the tangibility of that promise if you remain in faith. A Holy-Spirit-quickened word produces the faith for you to activate.

Sanctified Mind and Imagination

It is essential to be able to hear from God as this is the key to producing faith: "Faith comes from hearing, and hearing by the word of Christ" (Romans 10:17). Jesus said, "My sheep hear My voice . . . and they follow Me" (John 10:27).

God most often speaks to us through faint Spirit-inspired thoughts in our minds or images and impressions in our imagination. He created us in His own image and likeness, and that includes our minds and imaginations. He never intended that our minds and imaginations would host evil and vain thoughts or impressions, but rather that we would be one with His thoughts and visions. Receiving His revelation entails sanctifying (setting apart for God's purposes) these hidden faculties.

Sinful thoughts or impressions in your mind's eye (imagination) can taint your ability to hear accurately. As with a water reservoir, the water might be pure at its source but if there are contaminants in the pipes, the water will be compromised by the time it gets poured into a drinking glass.

Only if our lives are pure before the Lord and without mixture can we hear from God with accuracy.

Invite the Holy Spirit to convict you of any ungodly beliefs, thoughts, or images that are in your mind and imagination. Repent (which means turning away from sinful actions, words and thoughts and returning to God's ways) and receive forgiveness. First John 1:9 teaches that if we confess our sin, not only will He forgive us, but He will cleanse us from all unrighteousness. That clears the slate and we are ready to receive.

When you have a sanctified mind and imagination, you will be positioned to hear from the Holy Spirit. Then what you hear from the Spirit will produce faith.

The Secret Place

> When you pray, go into your room, and when you have shut your door, pray to your father who is in the secret place; and your father who sees in secret will reward you openly.
>
> Matthew 6:6 NKJV

The secret place is where you spend time alone in fellowship with God. There is no one as important as Him and there is no activity greater in life than spending time with Him. It is when you are alone with Him that He will reveal Himself to you—His love, His riches and His promises.

I set apart time daily to be with the Lord but I also carve out time at the end of each year to be with Him for extended times of prayer, worship and study of His Word. During one of those times away, God granted me a profound revelation regarding His glory and imparted to me an "author's anointing." I had never written a book previously and I was already in my fifties at the time. I was enjoying time with God in the "secret place" when the Holy Spirit spoke into my thoughts, "I want you to write a book on the Third Heaven." Shocked, I argued, "I am not an author—I have never written a book before and I would not know how."

The Holy Spirit responded, "But I am an Author, I have written a Book, and I know how! I authored the Scriptures and I can give you an author's anointing if you will receive it." The words He spoke into my thoughts that day produced faith, and by faith I received the "author's anointing" that day. Now I have written over 83 books, booklets, manuals and curriculums. The author's anointing is one of the riches of heaven that enables believers to bring the word and testimony of the Lord to the world we live in, and it is available to us through Christ.

Before Dr. Oral Roberts passed into glory, he personally invited a number of ministers into his home on a monthly basis to impart anointing to them. I had the honor of being his guest in one of these sessions. We were all invited to ask him one question each about his life or ministry. The question on my heart was, "Dr. Roberts, how did you manage to maintain a close walk with the Lord in the midst of all that you did as a television evangelist, apostle, author, builder of a university, Bible school, medical facility and multiple missions projects?"

He replied without hesitation, "Oh that was easy! I had my sacred time with God in my secret place every day. When I closed the door behind me, I was with God and no one was permitted to disturb me—not my wife, my children or even the President of the United States. No one and no task were more important to me than being with God. It was in the sacred place with God that He gave me every assignment and every revelation I was called to act on—it all came from that place. And once I said yes to Him, grace from heaven came on me to accomplish the task. It was easy." Dr. Roberts knew the riches that were available in the secret place.

Every fruitful minister has found the secret of the secret place (see Song of Solomon 2:14[2]). This is where the riches of heaven are imparted. This is where true faith is birthed.

Faith Is Vital

Without faith, you will not be enabled to "download" the promises of God that deliver the riches of heaven into your life here on earth. Faith is your vital key. Spend time in the presence of God, read His Word, invite the Holy Spirit to impart revelation to you that will produce faith and then *activate* your faith. Without action, your faith will not produce anything: "For just as the body without the spirit is dead, so also faith without works is dead" (James 2:26).

Your faith enables you to live in the realm of His heavenly riches—and yes, your faith will also enable you to ascend into the heavenly dimension and then bring blessings back with you into the earthly realm. To find out more about ascending and descending, turn to the next chapter.

SUMMARY

1. Faith is your heavenly currency. All the promises Jesus purchased on Calvary are in your "heavenly bank

account" and connecting to the promises of God with faith gives you the ability to make withdrawals from that account.

2. Facts are temporal; truth is eternal. Even when the facts may not yet seem to match the promises you believe by faith, God's truth *will* manifest itself.
3. Faith is evidence of what you have not yet seen; it is your internal reality. It is vital in order to live in the realm of His heavenly riches.
4. When you receive a Spirit-quickened word, it produces the faith in you to act upon it. A sanctified mind and time in the "secret place" will ensure you are hearing and interpreting correctly.

QUESTIONS TO PONDER

1. Can you think of a personal experience in which you acted upon a Spirit-quickened word? Did you struggle at first or immediately "just know"? What was the fruit?
2. What is the difference between begging God for something and standing in faith on His promises? What are your prayers most like?
3. A sanctified mind and imagination as well as personal time with the Lord are vital to both hearing and having the faith to act on His words. Do you have peace about your sanctification in these two areas? If not, what do you need to deal with? Are you ready and willing to? Why or why not?

MAKE THIS DECLARATION OVER YOUR LIFE

I have faith to access the riches of heaven. Faith is the substance of what I hope for and it is the evidence of what appears invisible to me. If the Word says it, I believe it and that settles it. Faith is birthed in me every time I hear the Holy Spirit speak to me. I have God's faith at work in my life.

7

Ascending and Descending

> Truly, truly, I say to you, you will see the heavens opened and the angels of God ascending and descending on the Son of Man.
>
> John 1:51

Every believer has both an invitation from the Lord to engage in divine encounters and legal permission through the finished work of the cross to access and enter the realm of heaven.

In the Bible we find indicators that heaven is "up" and the earth is beneath. For example, Jesus looked up toward heaven when He was praying to His Father regarding the loaves and the fish:

> Ordering the people to sit down on the grass, He took the five loaves and the two fish, and *looking up toward heaven,*

> He blessed the food, and breaking the loaves He gave them to the disciples, and the disciples gave them to the crowds.
>
> Matthew 14:19, emphasis added

He also looked up when He prayed for the one who was deaf:

> And *looking up to heaven* with a deep sigh, He said to him, "Ephphatha!" that is, "Be opened!"
>
> Mark 7:34, emphasis added

The Bible also speaks of "ascending" (going up) and "descending" (going down). At the beginning of His public ministry, Jesus exercised divine knowledge that amazed Nathanael. Jesus responded to his reaction of amazement with this prophetic statement:

> And He said to him, "Truly, truly, I say to you, you will see the heavens opened and the angels of God *ascending and descending* on the Son of Man."
>
> John 1:51, emphasis added

The angels of God ascended to heaven and descended from heaven in service to Jesus. If Jesus lives in you, then angelic service is rendered to you also, as you are in Christ.

We recall earlier confirmation of the action of angels ascending and descending in the life of Jacob:

> He had a dream, and behold, a ladder was set on the earth with its top reaching to heaven; and behold, the angels of God were *ascending and descending* on it. . . . Then Jacob awoke from his sleep and said, "Surely the LORD is in this place, and I did not know it." He was afraid and said, "How

> awesome is this place! This is none other than the house of God, and this is the gate of heaven."
>
> Genesis 28:12, 16–17, emphasis added

Not only did he see angels ascending and descending in his dream, he also received the revelation of his connection to heaven and that he was *the house of God* even as believers today are the temple of the Holy Spirit.[1] He was aware of the awesomeness of "this place" referring to the believer's life. We are *the house of God* when we come to Christ; we are to steward our lives as His temple with reverence, as holy unto the Lord.

It is assumed that the apostle Paul was referring to himself when he said "I know a man in Christ" who ascended and descended into heaven. Here is how he shared about it with the church at Corinth:

> I know a man in Christ who fourteen years ago—whether in the body I do not know, or out of the body I do not know, God knows—such a man was caught up to the third heaven.
>
> 2 Corinthians 12:2

We know according to his own testimony that he ascended, and of course he must have descended because fourteen years later he wrote to the church at Corinth concerning his experience. It is important to note also that just because Paul testified about this one instance does not mean that he had only one encounter in heaven. I believe that he could have ascended and descended regularly by the evidence of the various divine revelations he penned in Scripture.

Moses also ascended into heaven along with more than seventy others who were with him. Here is the account:

> Then Moses went up with Aaron, Nadab and Abihu, and seventy of the elders of Israel, and they saw the God of Israel; and under His feet there appeared to be a pavement of sapphire, as clear as the sky itself. Yet He did not stretch out His hand against the nobles of the sons of Israel; and they saw God, and they ate and drank.
>
> Exodus 24:9–11

Imagine how glorious it would have been for them to be in the presence of God in heaven on sapphire pavement, as well as eating and drinking in heaven. Moses and those who accompanied him obviously descended because he ministered further before God and the people of Israel in the wilderness following this encounter.

Many believe that only specially anointed and appointed ministers can ascend into heaven, but that is not true. Let's look at some Scriptures to reveal that this access is for every believer.

Hebrews 4:16, for example, exhorts believers to draw near with boldness to the throne of grace. Where is the throne of grace? It is in heaven. It is the throne that Jesus sits on—the mercy seat. It is not a throne in the earth; it is established in the heavens. Scripture confirms that Jesus sits in heaven at the right hand of the Father (see Ephesians 1:20). The writer of the letter to the Hebrews further reveals that when you are in heaven at the throne of grace, you can obtain things there (such as mercy and grace) and bring them back to minister into your need in the earthly dimension: "Therefore let us draw near with confidence to the throne of grace, so that we may receive mercy and find grace to help in time of need" (Hebrews 4:16).

The same writer also explains in another portion of Scripture that we "have already come . . . to the . . . heavenly Jerusalem" (Hebrews 12:22). He was not speaking to some choir in heaven; he was speaking to believers on the earth. Look at what you as a believer have "come to":

> But you have come to Mount Zion and to the city of the living God, the heavenly Jerusalem, and to myriads of angels, to the general assembly and church of the firstborn who are enrolled in heaven, and to God, the Judge of all, and to the spirits of the righteous made perfect, and to Jesus, the mediator of a new covenant, and to the sprinkled blood, which speaks better than the blood of Abel.
>
> Hebrews 12:22–24

How Do You Enter Heaven?

You will discover through the Scriptures that you enter by sincere faith. Faith is based on truth and not a feeling or a specific experience. The Word says you can stand before the throne of grace—so you *can*. You simply step forward by faith and stand in the heavenly dimension. Your faith establishes your experience, not your feelings or outward circumstances.

In the Old Testament, Moses was appointed by God to build a tabernacle in the wilderness. The study of the tabernacle is amazing, as it prophetically discloses and reveals Jesus and His finished work on the cross.[2] There was the gate in which God's people could enter, then the outer court in which there were a brazen altar and laver where the priests would offer the sacrifices God's people brought them and partake of special cleansing before going into the holy place.

The holy place hosted a table of shewbread and the golden lampstand. Only the priests could enter this place. They worshipped and interceded there and kept the lamps burning.

The holy of holies—the innermost place in the tabernacle, however, was where the glory of God was fully manifested. The ark of the covenant was situated there with the mercy seat upon it. Cherubim made of pure gold spread their wings over the mercy seat. God spoke concerning His people above the mercy seat between the wings of the cherubim. Only the high priest could enter this place, and only once a year to make atonement for the sins of the people.

There was a veil between the holy place and the holy of holies, which two thousand years ago was supernaturally rent from the top to the bottom when Christ was crucified.[3] It was a sign that Jesus had established the true and living tabernacle in heaven and had given all believers access. No longer did a veil separate us from God and His glorious presence. The true holy place—heaven itself—was available for every believer to enter. Through the gift of eternal life in Christ, we were given access to the eternal dimension and to God's holy domain—to the heavenly holy of holies.

> For Christ did not enter *a holy place made with hands*, a mere copy of the true one, but *into heaven itself*, now to appear in the presence of God for us.
>
> Hebrews 9:24, emphasis added

This Scripture explains that Jesus entered into heaven itself, not the natural tent in which was the holy of holies that Moses and his people built in the wilderness.

Now, because of Jesus' death and resurrection, any believer can enter the holiest place:

> Therefore, brethren, *since we have confidence to enter the holy place by the blood of Jesus*, by a new and living way which He inaugurated for us through the veil, that is, His flesh, and since we have a great priest over the house of God, *let us draw near with a sincere heart in full assurance of faith*, having our hearts sprinkled clean from an evil conscience and our bodies washed with pure water. Let us hold fast the confession of our hope without wavering, for He who promised is faithful.
>
> Hebrews 10:19–23, emphasis added

These verses are very exciting. The writer is declaring that we can have full confidence to enter the holy place *in heaven itself* through the finished work of the cross. Jesus gave us access. He goes on to exhort us to draw near to heaven itself ("the holy place") in full assurance of faith. You engage, you draw near, with your faith.

Through faith, I can boldly stand before God in the heavens and worship Him. I can also access promises and blessings and bring them into the earthly dimension by activating my faith as I am led and directed by the Holy Spirit. This is why Jesus taught us to pray for His Kingdom to come and His will to be done on earth as it is in heaven.

Personal Encounters

There are two types of heavenly encounters that can be experienced by believers: sovereign encounters and faith encounters. During a sovereign encounter, the individual has nothing to do with initiating it—it is God-initiated and God-fulfilled. A faith encounter, on the other hand, involves the believer's own faith laying hold of what God has already granted as promised and confirmed in His Word. The Scriptures reveal that "the righteous will live by his faith" (Habukkuk 2:4). Nowhere does it say that the righteous live by sovereign visitations! Still, the banquet table of promises to access heaven and to receive God's riches in heaven has now been set for everyone who believes, and both kinds of heavenly encounters are available to us.

In January of 1994, I experienced my first visitation into heaven. Prior to that, I did not even know that an individual could encounter heaven before dying, but God in His sovereignty took me into His heavenly abode. I heard audible sounds and voices, saw activities around the altar of God, viewed angelic assignments and was taken into open prophetic visions during my time there. It was a glorious experience and the Lord taught me many profound truths through it. Following that encounter, I constantly asked God for more heavenly visits, but to no avail.

Six years later, I picked up prophet Bob Jones from the airport in Kelowna, British Columbia, Canada, as he was one of the speakers at an event I was hosting. Bob was one of the most profound and accurate seers in our day. (He has since passed into his eternal glory, at a ripe old age.) On our way to the venue, I shared with him my heavenly visit in 1994. I knew he had experienced numerous visitations himself. I asked about them, and he replied, "Yep, I go to heaven every day—I call them my 'raptures.'"

My jaw dropped. What? Every day? I shared my desperation and deep longings to enjoy more encounters and how

I had been crying out for six years since my initial visit in 1994 without any manifestation of answered prayer. He said, "That is because you are asking for something you already have. Ephesians 2:6 says you are already seated in heavenly places in Christ, so what are you waiting for?" That response confused me. What did he mean by "what am I waiting for?"—I am waiting for God! He saw that I was perplexed and committed to praying for me the next day. I could hardly wait as I thought I would receive a great, supernatural impartation that would launch me into my own "daily raptures."

The next day I was filled with anticipation from the moment I awoke. After the morning session, we were in the lunchroom together. Bob was at my table so I took the opportunity to ask him more questions about heavenly visitation. He graciously answered and then asked, "Would ya like to go to heaven right now?" I was surprised but delighted. "You mean, right here in the lunchroom?" I inquired. He responded, "Yep."

I stood up as he took my hands. He explained that he was going to pray and that as he did, I would go to heaven. He continued to explain that while in heaven the Lord would give me something to bring back to earth. He told me that God would show me visions in my mind's eye to reveal to me what was transpiring in the heavenly encounter. He explained that the visions in my mind would be like a window into what God was doing with me in the heavenly dimension. I was so excited! Memories of my sovereign encounter in 1994 flooded back into my heart. I could hardly wait.

As I stood in eager expectation, he prayed and then told me that I would begin to see things. Well, in all honesty, I could not see a thing. My eyes were closed and all I could see was some shimmering light on the backdrop of my eyelids. There was a bank of windows in the room on my right with sunrays shining through, so I assumed that the shimmering light was from that, but as I focused on it, the faint image seemed to turn into a flame (at least that was what I was seeing in my mind's eye). As I was pondering this, Bob suddenly said, "So you're seeing the flickering flame, are ya?" I was surprised that he was declaring this faint image I was seeing in my mind's eye. Until then, I had not assumed that this image was anything from God, but his confirmation built my expectation.

As I continued to gaze upon the image in my mind's eye, I saw that I was actually becoming the flame. Again, Bob said, "So you've now become the flame, have ya?"

I was more than shocked to realize that he was aware of what was going on in the vision in my mind.

He then instructed, "Now, God is going to give you something to bring back to earth from heaven, so be on the alert to what He reveals to you." I questioned in my mind, "What? Bring back something from heaven?—I am not even in heaven yet." I was looking for the same kind of encounter I had in 1994 and this was definitely not it! I patiently remained in a receiving mode and saw a faint image in my mind's eye of snow-capped mountains and eagles soaring. I shared this image with Bob. He responded, "Yep, I had that vision in 1984. That is the emergence of the prophets in the Pacific Northwest." I was delighted that he had seen the same vision, but I did not believe it was anything I had brought back from heaven. The prayer time finished and that was that. What a disappointment. I still had not gone into heaven . . . or so I thought.

Shortly before that day in the lunchroom, Stacey Campbell, a respected prophetess, had been asked by Dr. Peter Wagner to establish a prophetic council in Canada. She asked if I would help her and I agreed to serve. At that time Canada lacked prophets who received words on a national level so we pulled as many "potentials" as we could find and even imported a few from the United States to help and support her mandate. On the first day of the council (which was six months following my encounter in the lunchroom), I was back at the airport in Kelowna, a city in the beautiful Pacific Northwest. It is situated in a valley with mountains encircling it, and it happened to be snowing on that particular day—yes, snow-capped mountains all around me. I was there picking up the prophets (eagles are often used to symbolize prophets) when the Lord said, "This day is the fulfillment of what you brought back from heaven six months ago"—snow-capped mountains and eagles!

God was informing me that the prophetic council He was establishing in Canada was actually brought from the heavenly dimension into the earth—and I had failed to realize it. It was similar to what Jacob expressed after he had his dream: "Surely the LORD is in this place; and I knew it not" (Genesis 28:16 KJV).

That particular prophetic council became a historic event in Canada. Following that first event, many prophets were identified in the nation, and the national prophetic council of prophets continued to grow along with many regional and provincial groups.

God moves in a variety of ways. Sometimes His ways are subtle, faint, and quiet, and other times dramatic and crystal clear. I had desired a dramatic, clear encounter like my sovereign visit to heaven in 1994, but God was teaching me how to access the heavenly realm with its bountiful riches by faith as I followed the Holy Spirit's faint nudges and impressions.

My grandson called me once when he was very young and said, "Grandma, did you know that just because something is invisible it doesn't mean it's not real?" I think we often fail to enjoy heavenly encounters because we have a predetermined perception of how God is going to meet with us, causing us to dismiss the faint and the invisible.

God is sovereign and He can initiate anything at any time, but He has not promised to give us sovereign dramatic encounters. He has, however, already given us everything through Christ—all that He is and all that He has. It can all be accessed by faith.

A dramatic sovereign encounter is not necessarily more anointed or authoritative than a faint encounter that you access by faith. They are just different kinds of encounters. You can always access the eternal truth by faith, but you cannot direct a sovereign encounter.

When you access an encounter by faith there is reward due to the exercise of your faith as you follow the Holy Spirit. Faith is what impresses God and it is what God rewards. Righteousness was reckoned unto Abraham because of his faith and Hebrews 11:6 confirms that "without faith it is impossible to please Him." A sovereign encounter, on the other hand, requires no initiation or exercise of faith by the individual, and therefore no eternal reward to the receiver although the blessing of the encounter is wonderful for the person.

Through God's sovereign plan, He gave us all that He is and all that He has. We have been granted all that pertains to life through His Son Jesus Christ. It is our responsibility now to exercise our faith to access what He has *already given*. It is our faith that impresses Him and it is our faith that He rewards.

I have heard believers say, "I am not going to heaven unless God comes in His sovereignty and takes me." Well, unfortunately, they might never experience heaven or its riches even though those blessings would always be available to them if they were to access this glorious God-realm by faith. You cannot tell God how He is going to encounter you. That was Thomas' problem. He did not want to believe unless he could touch Christ's wounds himself. Jesus was merciful but not impressed:

> So the other disciples were saying to him (Thomas), "We have seen the Lord!" But he (Thomas) said to them, "Unless I see in His hands the imprint of the nails, and put my finger into the place of the nails, and put my hand into His side, I will not believe."
>
> After eight days His disciples were again inside, and Thomas with them. Jesus came, the doors having been shut, and stood in their midst and said, "Peace be with you."
>
> Then He said to Thomas, "Reach here with your finger, and see My hands; and reach here your hand and put it into My side; and do not be unbelieving, but believing."
>
> Thomas answered and said to Him, "My Lord and my God!"
>
> Jesus said to him, "Because you have seen Me, have you believed? Blessed are they who did not see, and yet believed."
>
> John 20:25–29

So often we are looking for a tangible experience by which our natural senses can confirm the reality, but God is looking for faith. Faith in what is true is our internal reality. "Faith is the evidence" (Hebrews 11:1).

When I was new to understanding the reality of ascending into heaven by faith, I would intentionally activate my faith to ascend during times of worship. I had meditated on the worship that goes on endlessly in heaven, described in Revelation, chapters 4 and 5, and I had determined that if I could boldly access the throne, then I was going to worship God in heaven even though my physical body was on the earth. Like Jesus, I was going to be able to bilocate and stand in the earth and before the throne in heaven at the same time.

Worship in the Throne Room

One Sunday morning, I was worshipping God in a church service. By faith I stood before God in heaven to worship Him even though my body was standing in the church sanctuary. You might think, "Wow, that must feel very special to be in the throne room," but remember that faith is not always accompanied by feelings. I felt the same as I would have if I had not accessed the heavenly dimension in worship by faith. By faith, I stepped into the throne room and worshipped God. I believed I was before His throne worshipping Him. I was not standing in the earth trying to throw worship up to Him hoping that my efforts made it. No, I believed I was there regardless of feelings or senses I might or might not have. I was worshipping Him face-to-face—that was my internal reality! I believed we were engaged—again, that was my internal reality. Worshipping in the throne room by faith had become my regular practice, and to this day, I worship face-to-face by faith. In that sense, I can testify that I ascend every day.

On that particular Sunday as I was worshipping, completely focused on God, I saw an impression in my mind's eye. In the vision, I saw a fuel pump. It looked like an old-fashioned fuel pump with a sign on the top of it that said FRESH OIL. I saw a nozzle and a button that said FILL UP on the front of the pump. I felt the prompting of the Spirit of God as a prophetic act and response to take the nozzle and press it into my belly while pushing the button to receive a "fill-up." All this I saw in my mind's eye. I had not been trying to see this—I was happy to be completely focused on God in worship. I believe the Spirit of God led me into this place. Then the Spirit of God spoke into my thoughts, *This is the fueling room in heaven. I always want you to be filled with fresh oil. I do not want you to be like five foolish virgins who had no oil for their lamps. I always want you ready. You can come to this place whenever you want and receive fresh oil.*

Scripture must always support and confirm your spiritual encounters. On that day, I believe I was directed by the Spirit of God from the throne room where I was worshipping to the fueling room in heaven where I received fresh oil. I cannot remember a Scripture that supports the appearance of an old-fashioned gas pump with a nozzle or English signage. But there is a Scripture in Zechariah 4:11–12 that supports oil pipes and distribution of the oil in a heavenly vision:

> Then I said to him, "What are these two olive trees on the right of the lampstand and on its left?" And I answered the second time and said to him, "What are the two olive

> branches which are beside the two golden pipes, which empty the golden oil from themselves?"

Once you receive a revelation from the Spirit of God, it has your name on it—it belongs to you and to your descendants. Deuteronomy 29:29 declares: "The secret things belong to the LORD our God, but the things revealed belong to us and to our sons forever, that we may observe all the words of this law."

The fueling room in heaven that I described to you is a room I have access to because the Holy Spirit revealed it to me. I know the room experientially and I am responsible to steward the revelation. After I ascend to receive a fresh infilling by faith, I descend and bring the fresh oil (anointing) with me. It does not matter if others believe it or not. They can question it, they can scorn me or ridicule me, but I cannot be moved from the reality of the encounter. My faith is the substance and evidence of this encounter. I am now familiar with many rooms and locations in heaven and I have had many authentic and fruit-bearing faith encounters directed by the Holy Spirit. You can, too.

The apostle Paul wrote, "For I received from the Lord that which I also delivered to you, that the Lord Jesus in the night in which He was betrayed took bread " (1 Corinthians 11: 23).

I find this interesting because Paul was not there on the night Jesus was betrayed, so where did he receive the detailed insight of the betrayal? We know from 2 Corinthians 12:4 that Paul ascended into heaven. I am convinced that Jesus likely revealed the night of the betrayal and other teachings to him while Paul was in a heavenly encounter. For sure, whatever Paul received, he then delivered to the people, having quite possibly ascended to receive the revelation and insight and descended with the revelation to share with others.

How to Ascend and Descend by Faith

You might be longing to ascend and descend but you are not quite sure how to launch. The following are keys of understanding to help you.

1. **The Holy Spirit is God's gift to you.** The Holy Spirit is God's Spirit who is with you always. He will lead and guide you into all truth and reveal all that has been given to you in Christ. Invite Him to fill you afresh and lead you into divine encounter in the heavens. Yield to Him. You are not going to direct your own encounter—He will. When you make the decision to yield, He will lead you regardless of what you feel or sense. (See John 16:13–14 and Romans 8:14.)
2. **Sanctify your mind and imagination.** The Holy Spirit commonly speaks to believers through their thoughts and faint images in the imagination. He will reveal to you the things He wants you to see and understand as you receive His thoughts and images, no matter how faint they might be. Cast down any vain imaginations that come from your carnal nature and in Jesus' name bind the enemy from interfering. A sanctified mind and imagination are *set apart* for God. That is what *sanctify* means. Ask the Lord to cleanse you from any defiling thoughts or images that you have allowed in your soul and He will purify you. (See Matthew 16:19, 2 Corinthians 10:3–5 and 1 John 1:9.)

3. **Stand on the Word.** The Word will reveal to you what is reality in the invisible realm. For example, we have already studied that we have invitation and exhortation to approach the throne of grace in heaven with boldness and to obtain what we are seeking. That is the truth. When you stand on that Word, you can then access the throne of grace through your faith. The Holy Spirit witnesses to your access. When your faith causes you to stand before the throne of grace, you have ascended regardless of what you feel or experience, yet every experience should be backed up by the Word. If your encounter is confirmed by the Word, it is authentic, for the Word is truth. (See Hebrews 4:16; John 17:17.)
4. **Ascend and descend by faith.** Except in the case of a sovereign activation by God, all your ascending and descending will be as a result of actuating your faith. As you ascend, the Spirit of God will reveal spiritual realities to you primarily through thoughts and images in your sanctified mind and imagination. As you descend, you have an invitation to bring those spiritual realities from the heavens into the realm of natural earth. For example, Hebrews 4:16 mentions that we can "obtain" mercy and receive grace to help in the earthly dimension. By faith, you intentionally bring back into the earth what was revealed to you in heaven. (See Hebrews 11:1.)
5. **Journal.** It is helpful to journal your ascending and descending encounters so that you can meditate on what the Lord has revealed to you and also measure the fruit that comes from the encounters. All authentic encounters in the heavenlies should produce measurable results

and fruit over time. The Bible is God's journal; He encourages journaling! (See Habakkuk 2:2.)

6. **Ascend and descend frequently.** The more you ascend and descend, the more sensitive you will become to the Spirit's leading and the more experiences you will enjoy. You will always grow through practice. (See Hebrews 5:14.)
7. **Be intentional.** I have discovered that the more I intentionally position myself to access heaven by faith, the more sensitive I become. Eventually, even when I am not looking for encounter, I have them. Your focus will create a realm of supernatural activity. (See Philippians 2:2.)
8. **Try it!** Try stepping into a heavenly encounter led by the Holy Spirit right now. Activate your faith and see what happens! If you are having trouble, you will find another great key in the next chapter.

SUMMARY

1. Through faith, you and I can boldly stand before God in the heavens and worship Him. We can also access promises and blessings and bring them into the earthly dimension by activating our faith as we are led and directed by the Holy Spirit.
2. In other words, as believers we have both an invitation from the Lord to engage in divine encounters and legal permission through the finished work of the cross to access and enter the realm of heaven. For example, the

Scriptures exhort us to have boldness to draw near to the throne of grace and to enter the Holy Place—both of which are heaven.

3. Not only Jesus, but also Moses and Paul as well as others, ascended into heaven at different times while they lived on earth. Like them, we can be bilocational.
4. There are two kinds of encounters: sovereign encounters, where you are taken to the heavens by God's initiative, and faith encounters, where you, by faith, access the heavenly realm. One experience is not superior to the other.
5. These encounters in heaven can give us, among other things, revelation and insight, prophetic words, strength, confidence, and, as in my own personal experience, an opportunity to refuel with fresh oil.
6. Believe that this is God's gift to you and His Word is truth. Sanctify your mind, then ascend and descend by faith. Do this with intentionality. The more frequently you ascend and descend, the more sensitive you will become to the leading of the Holy Spirit. Journal your experiences in order to meditate on what the Lord has revealed to you.

QUESTIONS TO PONDER

1. Is this understanding that you can—and should—ascend and descend into heaven a new concept to you? How have the Scriptures here helped you to understand this invitation?

2. Have you had experiences ascending and descending into heaven? How did they impact you? Did you bring back something to share with others?
3. If you never have before, are you ready to accept the invitation at the end of this chapter to step into a heavenly encounter right now? Why or why not? Journal your experience.

MAKE THIS DECLARATION OVER YOUR LIFE

I have faith to access the realm of heaven and engage in heavenly encounters. I believe His Word, which tells me I have legal permission to enter into the Holy Place through the finished work of the cross. I accept His invitation and confidently approach the Throne of grace, where I can receive mercy, grace and so much more.

8

Accessing Riches in Heaven through Praise and Worship

> Be exalted, O God, above the heavens; let Your glory be above all the earth.
>
> Psalm 57:5 NKJV

A number of years ago, my ministry was hosting a conference in Phoenix, Arizona. The praise and worship the first evening were dynamic, and we were all very aware of the tangible, weighty presence of God in the gathering. Suddenly, during the worship, I felt a shift in the spirit. It was as though the heavens opened over us and a powerful atmosphere of supernatural faith moved in. Unexpectedly, a blast of sparkling sapphire-colored dust fell on the front row where the speakers were sitting. My Bible was open and the pages were covered with this rich blue glory manifestation. Others had the sapphire dust on their clothing, skin and hair. We were all in awe. We knew a portal had opened and that God was pouring out His heavenly riches upon us. It was a sign and a wonder!

After the meeting, a number of us were in the green room celebrating and fellowshipping. One of our friends had brought a guest with him who was not a Christian yet. This Jewish gentleman had attended the meeting and had witnessed the sparkling sapphire dust. He was very skeptical and he suggested to me that possibly someone had thrown around some glitter from the dollar store. As I was listening to him, a vision of a big ball of sapphire-colored glitter came into view. It moved right in front of him and then burst open. Once again, there was sapphire glitter everywhere. The weight of the glory presence became very heavy and joy filled our hearts. It was undeniable that God was in our midst and that He was demonstrating His heavenly glory. The Jewish gentleman was shocked and awe-filled. Needless to say, he became a believer that night. The Scripture says that "the Jews require a sign" (1 Corinthians 1:22 KJV)—well, God gave it to him and it was effective.

Over the weekend we had many manifestations of heavenly glory in the midst of our praise and worship as well as during the preaching of the Word, including the supernatural release of heavenly oil, supernatural healings, powerful prophetic flows, and falling gold- and silver-colored glory dust. A portal into heavenly riches and glory opened wide over the meetings.

Many believers struggle with signs and wonders. Not only do some not believe when they hear about them; many oppose them outright. "Why on earth would God send glitter into a meeting?" they might ask. One time, God was pouring out feathers in a meeting. Feathers filled the room. It was very exciting, but one agitated attendee complained, "This is nonsense! Why would God fill the room with feathers?" The revivalist who was leading the meeting responded, "If you have trouble with a feather, you would really have a problem with a whole angel!"

Such heavenly signs are meant to point you to the sphere of the supernatural, and ultimately they point you to the God of the supernatural, to Jesus, with amazement and awe. When heaven invades earth, things happen!

The signs are not to be worshipped, of course. When I am driving someplace where I am scheduled to minister and I catch sight of a sign pointing me to the correct street, I am elated at the confirmation, but that sign is not my destination. Its purpose is to point me in the right direction. I would never think of getting out of my car and bowing down in front of the sign to worship it. Signs and wonders (called that because wonders make you wonder) get our attention to show us that heaven is in our midst.

Heavenly Portals

A heavenly portal is a window, door or opening into God's realm. In Christ, we can live under an open heaven; He opened the way for us. That is why when we are in gatherings and the heavens are opened over us, His Kingdom invades the room. Let's review some Scriptures that will bring confirmation to you regarding the open heaven that you are invited to live under.

The LORD will *open for you His good storehouse, the heavens*, to give rain to your land in its season and to bless all the work of your hand; and you shall lend to many nations, but you shall not borrow.

Deuteronomy 28:12, emphasis added

After being baptized, Jesus came up immediately from the water; and behold, the *heavens were opened*, and he saw the Spirit of God descending as a dove and lighting on Him.

Matthew 3:16, emphasis added

And He said to him, "Truly, truly, I say to you, you will see the *heavens opened* and the angels of God ascending and descending on the Son of Man."

John 1:51, emphasis added

But being full of the Holy Spirit, he [Stephen] gazed intently into heaven and saw the glory of God, and Jesus standing at the right hand of God; and he said, "Behold, I see *the heavens opened* up and the Son of Man standing at the right hand of God."

Acts 7:55–56, emphasis added

Bring the whole tithe into the storehouse, so that there may be food in My house, and test Me now in this," says the LORD of hosts, "if I will not *open for you the windows of heaven* and pour out for you a blessing until it overflows."

Malachi 3:10, emphasis added

After these things I looked, and behold, a *door standing open in heaven*, and the first voice which I had heard, like the sound of a trumpet speaking with me, said, "Come up here, and I will show you what must take place after these things."

Revelation 4:1, emphasis added

The late Ruth Ward Heflin was a woman who lived under an open heaven. In her camp meetings, the heavens would open during praise and worship and the tangible weighty glory of God would manifest itself in a variety of signs, wonders and miracles.

In her book, *Glory—Experiencing the Atmosphere of Heaven*, she presented these memorable lines:[1]

Praise . . . until the Spirit of worship comes.
Worship . . . until the glory comes.
Then . . . Stand in the glory!

Praise That Opens the Heavens

As a minister, I have the blessing to lead church services and conferences that we host. I realize how vital it is to create an atmosphere of praise and celebration and I am honored to work with amazing worship leaders who understand the importance of exalting God in His majesty, power and presence. A worship service is not simply a nice way to bring the people together or a prelude to the preaching of the Word. As we begin with praise, it actually changes the atmosphere and causes people's gaze to be focused on the Lord.

Portals That Open in Corporate Gatherings

During corporate praise I am sensitive to when a heavenly portal opens. Often, when a portal opens I can sense angelic movement and hear the Spirit's directions for how to lead in the open heaven environment. Sometimes He will direct me to prophesy or to minister His presence and gifts, and sometimes I will be led to do nothing but personally celebrate the opening of the portal within my heart as I invite Him to increase His presence. When you step into the open portal, His presence escalates. When a portal opens you can sense the Spirit capturing the attention of His people, and He individually begins to draw their hearts closer to His heart.

The Hebrew word *tehillah* refers to songs or hymns of adoration and thanksgiving to God in a public gathering.[2] Such praise calls forth awesome wonders in the midst of the people, things that are observable by all. "He is your praise [*tehillah*] and He is your God, who has done these great and awesome things for you which your eyes have seen" (Deuteronomy 10:21). When we praise God corporately, a portal opens and God moves.

We also get an idea of how corporate praise is connected to God's greatness and the subsequent manifestation of His miracles in the New Testament. Praise can produce open portals that bring about miraculous occurrences, but praise can also be a response to miraculous occurrences, and in these cases, the portal will enlarge and the power will increase. One New Testament word for praise is the Greek word *aineō*, which means "to praise, extol, to sing praises in honor to God."[3]

Praise and miracles are often found together. Luke records a time (one of many) when Jesus was in the midst of a crowd that was praising God joyfully and loudly. As they praised, they acknowledged the miracles they had witnessed: "As soon as He was approaching, near the descent of the Mount of Olives, the whole crowd of the disciples began to praise God joyfully with a loud voice for all the miracles which they had seen" (Luke 19:37).

I was recently at a gathering where powerful praise was released during a morning meeting. Many were singing, dancing and rejoicing in the Lord with passionate shouts and proclamations. The praise continued to escalate and the whole atmosphere became filled with His mighty presence. I could feel a portal open. At that moment the leader of the meeting, discerning the open portal, went forward and began to prophesy dynamic and detailed prophetic words. A number of people were invited to the front to receive, and the glory of God hit them so powerfully that the entire prayer line went down like dominoes under the Spirit's weighty glory.

Corporate praise releases the power of God in tangible ways.

Portals That Open in Personal Devotions

Portals also open during the praise you offer in your personal devotion times. A while ago, I was facing a situation in which I needed the wisdom of God. I prayed, read the Word and took counsel with some other leaders, but I could not seem to connect with the wisdom that was needed to resolve the situation. One day in my personal time with the Lord as I was striving to hear a solution from Him, I felt the Lord say, "Just praise Me." I moved my focus off the situation and onto Him, praising Him for all He is and for all He does. I walked around the room shouting my praise and proclaiming His excellence. After about fifteen minutes of focused, passionate praise, I felt a portal open and suddenly the solution filled my thoughts. Praise had opened the portal. I applied the wisdom I had received and the situation was settled.

Praise Changes the Atmosphere

In Acts 16:22–24 we read about the time when Paul and Silas were persecuted for their faith. Their robes were torn off them, and then they were beaten with rods and thrown into the inner prison with their feet fastened in stocks. That is what I would call a "bad day." It would be easy to feel the weight of the injustice and to moan and groan because of it, but Paul and Silas knew how to connect with heaven. Here is what they did:

> But about midnight Paul and Silas were praying and singing hymns of praise to God, and the prisoners were listening to them; and suddenly there came a great earthquake, so that the foundations of the prison house were shaken; and immediately all the doors were opened and everyone's chains were unfastened.
>
> Acts 16:25–26

I believe it is accurate to say that "praise changed the atmosphere." The Greek word for praise used in this passage is *hymneō*, meaning "to sing the praise of or to sing hymns to."[4]

A portal had opened and the power of heaven became manifest in the midst of their praise. Not only were the doors of their cell opened and their chains unfastened, but everyone in the prison was set free. The jailer, fearing the consequences he would suffer under his superiors for the escape of his prisoners, was about to kill himself, but Paul cried out to him and offered salvation for him and his entire household (see verses 27–31).

I have seen praise change the atmosphere many times. Years ago, the church I attended met in an Elks lodge. The room where we gathered on Sunday mornings regularly hosted an open bar and dancing on Saturday nights. I would go in early to pray, many hours before the service started. The atmosphere was oppressive, and you could smell the stale beer and cigarette smoke from the night before. Of course, I opened all the doors and windows I could, but the place needed more than some fresh air—it needed an atmospheric change. I would put on praise and worship music and begin to exalt the Lord with high praise. I was the only one there so I would praise with everything I had within me. Usually, after about an hour or so, I would feel the heavens opening and the presence of the Lord settling into the room. I loved preparing that room for God. As a result, our services were filled with wonderful corporate worship, prophetic words and miracles. It all began in a one-on-one time with God.

Open Up Ye Gates

Praise opens heavenly gates and releases the King of glory, who is a warrior battling on our behalf:

> Lift up your heads, O gates, and be lifted up, O ancient doors, that the King of glory may come in!
>
> Who is the King of glory? The Lord strong and mighty, the Lord mighty in battle.
>
> Lift up your heads, O gates, and lift them up, O ancient doors, that the King of glory may come in!
>
> Who is this King of glory? the Lord of hosts, He is the King of glory.
>
> Psalm 24:7–10

When he was faced with three enemy armies who outnumbered the troops of Israel, King Jehoshaphat experienced this in a powerful way. Having sought the Lord earnestly, he and his people put their whole trust in God for victory. Jehoshaphat led them in heartfelt praise and worship, and he appointed singers and worshippers to offer sustained praise during the battle. "When they began singing and praising, the LORD set ambushes against the sons of Ammon, Moab and Mount Seir, who had come against Judah; so they were routed" (2 Chronicles 20:22). Praise opened the way for God to prevail on the battlefield decisively.

I was on a mission outreach in Africa years ago, and one night after going to bed I was suddenly attacked with an assault from witchcraft. (A few satanic covens in the region deliberately targeted Christian ministers.) I could not move or speak as I lay there, but felt directed by the Spirit of God to speak the name of Jesus. I forced His name through my locked jaws and lips and immediately my body was loosed. I praised Him and glorified His name. After a few minutes of praising Him, I heard a scream outside and the sound of someone running quickly away from the compound where I was staying. Praise had opened the gate for the King of glory to come in and to prevail over evil forces. Later that week, members of the coven received the Lord at a miracle service.

Praise until the Spirit of Worship Comes

As you spend time praising God with exuberance for who He is and for what He does, you will find your heart at some point going into a deeper adoration of Him. It is like gazing face-to-face—a deep heart-to-heart connection. This is worship. Praise will take you into worship. When you are in worship, the atmosphere is different. It is reverent and without distraction.

Worship until the Glory Comes

God is seeking those who will worship Him (see John 4:23–24[5]). When you are in worship, you shift from thinking about your problems and frustrations into an undistracted focus on Him. He is all that matters—everything else grows dim. In this place of heart connection, born out of your sincere love for Him, God will fill your soul with Himself. You will become entwined with Him. As you linger in worship, you might experience the riches of His love and intimate adoration in ways that you have never known before.

As you remain in worship, you will suddenly be lost in it, finding yourself aware of the great weight of His presence—His glory.

Stand in the Glory

Oh, the glory! The glory is the realm of God—the realm of eternity. God *is* the glory. Various manifestations of His glory may include the glory of His beauty and radiance, the glory of healing, the glory of His provision, the glory of His wisdom and the glory of His power. Any time there is an atmosphere filled with His presence that manifests who He is, what He does, and what He has, that is the glory.

The many manifestations of the glory presence of God include a glory cloud and mist such as Israel encountered when they were in the wilderness and also when the priests worshipped at the dedication of Solomon's temple. I have seen the fire and the smoke such as what Isaiah saw when he was in the throne room (see Isaiah 6:1–4). I have encountered angelic presence in the glory along with many signs and wonders from God's dimension, such as heavenly winds, feathers falling, gold dust, heavenly fragrances and so on.

The Key Is Always within Your Grasp

When the heavy weight of God's presence comes in worship, you do not want to move. In this place of His presence you behold Him, the riches of His power, the riches of His glory. And you are transformed.

The apostle Paul explained this transformation that takes place in the glory: "But we all, with unveiled face, beholding as in a mirror the glory of the Lord, are being transformed into the same image from glory to glory, just as from the Lord, the Spirit" (2 Corinthians 3:18).

Together, praise and worship is a key to unlocking the riches of heaven, and this key is always within your grasp. Praise and worship will open heavenly portals, allowing you to live in the atmosphere of His glory. Set apart time to truly gaze upon Him and then lavish Him with the deepest adoration that you have within you. Then you can engage in the riches of His love and grace and be transformed into His likeness.

Yet there is more. We can have amazing, life-altering experiences under an open heaven through praise and worship, but to truly experience all the riches of heaven and to make an impact on the world with them, the key detailed in the following chapter is essential.

SUMMARY

1. Praise and worship open up the heavens, opening up portals and bringing about powerful signs and wonders.
2. The signs and wonders are not to be worshipped. Rather they are sent to get our attention and to show us that heaven is in our midst.
3. A heavenly portal is a window, door or opening into the realm of God. When the heavens are opened over us, His Kingdom invades the room. His presence escalates and His Spirit captures the attention of His people, drawing their hearts closer to His heart and allowing them to experience the glory of God in many ways.
4. Portals can also open during the praise and worship you offer in your personal devotion times. In such times of personal encounter with the Lord, you can receive wisdom, encouragement and more.
5. Praise also changes atmospheres and brings victory in warfare situations.
6. Therefore, praise until the spirit of worship comes. Worship until the glory comes. Stand in the glory!

QUESTIONS TO PONDER

1. Do you experience a lifestyle of praise and worship, or is it something you only engage in corporately? How has this chapter encouraged you to integrate praise and worship into your daily life?
2. Try to recall a powerful worship service you attended in which the heavens opened up. What led up to the

moment? What occurred as a result? How were you personally impacted?

3. Have you used praise as a means of warfare in the midst of spiritual battles? What has been the outcome?

MAKE THIS DECLARATION OVER YOUR LIFE

I have the key of praise and worship to unlock the riches of heaven. With this key I open up heavenly portals and experience the atmosphere of His glory. As I worship He fills my soul with more of Him. I engage in the riches of His love and grace so that I become transformed into His likeness and experience the great weight of His presence, His glory and its manifestations. I am ready and eager to experience His glory realm!

9

Be Spiritual

> For to be carnally minded is death, but to be spiritually minded is life and peace.
>
> Romans 8:6 NKJV

When Jesus came to earth and began His ministry, He preached the Kingdom of God, taught the Kingdom of God and demonstrated the Kingdom of God. The Spirit of God descended upon Him at His water baptism[1] and He never ministered without the demonstration of the power of the Holy Spirit. Jesus was not focused on or motivated by the natural. He was in the world but not of the world. He was deeply spiritual, committed to doing on the earth only the things He saw His Father do in heaven. Jesus' life and ministry was truly "heaven to earth."

He taught His disciples not to live as the Gentiles who were worried about natural things but to seek first the Kingdom of God:

> Do not worry then, saying, "What will we eat?" or "What will we drink?" or "What will we wear for clothing?" For the Gentiles eagerly seek all these things; for your heavenly Father knows that you need all these things. But seek first His kingdom and His righteousness, and all these things will be added to you."
>
> Matthew 6:31–33

Numerous times He carefully explained to His disciples that they had been commissioned to do the works that He did, and even greater works. As the Father had sent Him, they were also being sent. He was the example that they were to follow as they preached the good news of the Kingdom and demonstrated divine power.

> Truly, truly, I say to you, he who believes in Me, the works that I do, he will do also; and greater works than these he will do; because I go to the Father.
>
> John 14:12

> So Jesus said to them again, "Peace be with you; as the Father has sent Me, I also send you."
>
> John 20:21

> And as you go, preach, saying, "The kingdom of heaven is at hand." Heal the sick, raise the dead, cleanse the lepers, cast out demons. Freely you received, freely give.
>
> Matthew 10:7–8

> And He said to them, "Go into all the world and preach the gospel to all creation. . . .
>
> "These signs will accompany those who have believed: in My name they will cast out demons, they will speak with new tongues; they will pick up serpents, and if they drink any deadly poison, it will not hurt them; they will lay hands on the sick, and they will recover."
>
> So then, when the Lord Jesus had spoken to them, He was received up into heaven and sat down at the right hand of God.
>
> And they went out and preached everywhere, while the Lord worked with them, and confirmed the word by the signs that followed.
>
> Mark 16:15, 17–20

> I do not ask You to take them out of the world, but to keep them from the evil one. They are not of the world, even as I am not of the world.
>
> John 17:15–16

It is clear throughout the gospels that Jesus came to prepare His Church to be spiritually focused, demonstrating the power of the Spirit and bringing heaven to earth. As we look at the worldwide Church today, it is not difficult to recognize the fact that only a small percentage of believers are spiritually focused. Many are void of the Spirit, building the Church on social and community programs, but without demonstration of the Spirit and His power, and void of the atmosphere of heavenly glory. In some churches, the Scriptures are not even read in public meetings—only stories are told to highlight a point. Of course, there is nothing wrong with offering the community wholesome programs and sharing a good story to confirm God's Word, but we cannot ignore the Holy Spirit and His power—we must make Him central.

True spiritual believers will regularly experience and minister healings, deliverances, prophetic words and dreams; they will speak in tongues and enjoy encounters in the glory realm. This is normal for the spiritual Christian, and yet often you find such believers scorned for their passion and "extreme" spirituality by those who are not familiar with Kingdom life and power.

When Jesus left His disciples before His ascension, He told them to go to Jerusalem until they were clothed in power. It was important to Him that His Church would be spiritual and filled with power. He said, "And behold, I am sending forth the promise of My Father upon you; but you are to stay in the city until you are clothed with power from on high" (Luke 24:49).

In the book of Acts, we read about what happened next. It is another confirmation of what Jesus told His disciples, namely that, when the Holy Spirit came upon them, they would have power to be His witnesses on the earth: "But you will receive power when the Holy Spirit has come upon you; and you shall be My witnesses both in Jerusalem, and in all Judea and Samaria, and even to the remotest part of the earth" (Acts 1:8).

The *power* they were to receive is translated from a Greek word, *dynamis*,[2] which means "strength, power, ability," and that includes:

- inherent power . . .
- power for performing miracles

- moral power and excellence of soul
- the power and influence which belong to riches and wealth
- power and resources arising from numbers
- power consisting in or resting upon armies, forces, hosts

The heaven-inspired word *dynamis* describes miraculous power and supernatural ability from God. This is what Jesus wanted His Church clothed with. With this *dynamis* power we can access the riches of heaven and minister to the needy of the earth.

Before he was converted, the apostle Paul was a very zealous, respected religious leader, committed to obeying the Law of Moses and studying the Scriptures, but he was void of the Spirit and power. He persecuted the early Church, but he had a turnaround after his conversion, unashamedly teaching a radical new belief:

> For the word of the cross is foolishness to those who are perishing, but to us who are being saved it is the power of God. . . . But to those who are the called, both Jews and Greeks, Christ the power of God and the wisdom of God.
>
> 1 Corinthians 1:18, 24

> My message and my preaching were not in persuasive words of wisdom, but in demonstration of the Spirit and of power, so that your faith would not rest on the wisdom of men, but on the power of God.
>
> 1 Corinthians 2:4–5

> For the kingdom of God does not consist in words but in power.
>
> 1 Corinthians 4:20

Paul, prior to his conversion, was not a spiritual man. He was a religious man, and there is a difference. Religion consists of a person's own efforts and evaluations. Religion creates pressure for people to please God in their own strength rather than to receive by faith all God has given to every believer. Religion will restrain the manifestation of the Spirit. Religion creates self-righteousness in people and makes them in turn attempt to fulfill standards of godliness with their behavior, human efforts and actions.

Self-righteousness is born of the flesh in the same way that unrighteousness is. Works of immorality, lies, idolatry and so forth are unrighteous works of the flesh, along with self-righteousness. The fact is that neither self-righteousness nor unrighteousness can be tolerated in the lives of true believers.

A church without power is subject to being led by the flesh. Look at what Paul said regarding this:

> The mind set on the flesh is hostile toward God; for it does not subject itself to the law of God, for it is not even able to do so, and those who are in the flesh cannot please God.
>
> Romans 8:7–8

> Those who are motivated by the flesh only pursue what benefits themselves. But those who live by the impulses of the Holy Spirit are motivated to pursue spiritual realities. For the mind-set of the flesh is death, but the mind-set controlled by the Spirit finds life and peace. In fact, the mind-set focused on the flesh fights God's plan and refuses to submit to His direction, because it cannot! For no matter how hard they try, God finds no pleasure with those who are controlled by the flesh.

> But when the Spirit of Christ empowers your life, you are not dominated by the flesh but by the Spirit. And if you are not joined to the Spirit of the Anointed One, you are not of Him.
>
> Romans 8:5–9 TPT

To Be Spiritual, You Must Be Filled with the Holy Spirit

The apostle Paul describes to us the difference between a natural man and a spiritual man.

> Now we have received, not the spirit of the world, but the Spirit who is from God, that we might know the things that have been freely given to us by God. These things we also speak, not in words which man's wisdom teaches but which the Holy Spirit teaches, comparing spiritual things with spiritual. But the natural man does not receive the things of the Spirit of God, for they are foolishness to him; nor can he know them, because they are spiritually discerned.
>
> 1 Corinthians 2:12–14 NKJV

If we are going to receive from God and enjoy continual access to His heavenly riches, we must welcome the Holy Spirit to have first place in our lives. The Holy Spirit is "God with us." He is not a mere influence or power. He is the very Spirit of God sent by the Father to be with you.

On one occasion I had a vision of the Holy Spirit sitting outside a church against its wall. His head was down. In the encounter, I asked Him, "What are You doing here outside the church?" He looked up and responded, "They do not want me in there. I am waiting patiently until they do." I wept. He deserves His rightful place in our lives and in His

Church, but He fills only those who invite Him, honor Him and give Him a place to come in their hearts.

Baptized with the Holy Spirit

John the Baptist came to baptize with water unto repentance, but he said of Jesus, "He will baptize you with the Holy Spirit" (Matthew 3:11). The word "baptize" means "to be completely immersed or completely filled." It does not imply just a little dab, but rather fullness. I heard a preacher once share that the word *baptizo* was used in an ancient Greek pickling recipe. When you put a cucumber into the brine, eventually the cucumber transforms because it is "baptized" or fully immersed in the brine. That is what happens to us when we are saturated with the Spirit—we are transformed into the very image and likeness of God.

Another one of the meanings of the Greek word *baptizo* is "to dip repeatedly."[3] Let's constantly dip and be filled. Living full of the Holy Spirit will empower us to live a heavenly life in the earth.

In chapter 2 of the book of Acts, we find the account of the outpouring of the Spirit on the Day of Pentecost. All the believers who were there were filled with the Holy Spirit and all spoke in tongues. The whole Church was full of the Holy Spirit when it was birthed, and that is what God is looking for today. The early Church, saturated with the Spirit, won thousands to the Lord daily and moved in power. The book of Acts is not a boring book—it is a book of heavenly activity, miracles, signs, wonders and angelic visitations. If the book of Acts is to continue through God's Church today, let's keep writing it!

Benefits of Being Baptized with the Holy Spirit

When you are baptized with the Holy Spirit:

1. You receive heavenly *dynamis* power to activate miracles (see Acts 1:8).
2. You receive holy boldness to preach the Gospel (see Acts 4:31).
3. You receive the gifts of the Holy Spirit (see 1 Corinthians 12:4–11).
4. You have access to the open heaven (see Matthew 3:16).
5. You become a witness of Jesus Christ (see Acts 1:8).
6. You will mature and grow in the things of God (see Romans 8:14).
7. You will be guided into all truth (see John 16:13).
8. You will receive revelation of eternal truth (see John 16:15).
9. You will have insight into the future (see John 16:13).
10. You will be anointed (see Acts 10:38).

The bottom line is this: To be spiritual, you need to be baptized with the Holy Spirit.

Praying in Tongues

When you have the Holy Spirit, you also have His gifts, and one of His gifts is the gift of tongues, the gift of a spiritual language. When you speak in tongues, you do not understand what you are saying because the language is unknown to your natural mind, but it empowers your spiritual nature.

The gift of tongues is received and released by faith. The gifts of the Holy Spirit are inherent in Him and if He lives in you so do His gifts. You just have to let them out. Jesus said that out of our belly (innermost being) will flow rivers of living water (see John 7:38 KJV). He was speaking of the Spirit. Every believer can speak with tongues and should. Jesus said it is a sign that will follow those who believe. If you believe, you should speak with tongues.

Benefits of Praying in Tongues

1. You will be personally spiritually empowered and edified (see 1 Corinthians 14:4).
2. You will enter a realm of understanding divine mysteries (see 1 Corinthians 14:2).
3. You will pray perfect prayers that reflect heaven's agenda (see Romans 8:26–27).
4. You will empower God's holy faith within you (see Jude 20).
5. You will keep yourself in the love of God (see Jude 21).

When I received the gift of tongues as a new believer, I would pray in tongues for hours at a time—often continuously for six to eight hours. As a result, the supernatural realm has always felt natural to me, even as a brand-new Christian. Even back then, I experienced a holy boldness; I witnessed constantly and led many people to Christ. I cannot remember a time in the Lord when I did not receive fresh prophetic revelation, vision and boldness. The heavenly portals have been open over my life even though I have not understood the full dynamics of them all the time. I believe it happened because I prayed in tongues so much. To this day, I often experience prophetic and heavenly encounters while praying in tongues.

Tongues have always been a blessed part of my spiritual life to the point that I wonder how any believer can get through life victoriously without this gift. If you read this and it makes you hungry to be filled with the Spirit and released in tongues, then go before God and receive. It happens by faith, not by feelings.

We read in the book of Acts that "they were all filled with the Holy Spirit and began to speak with other tongues, as the Spirit was giving them utterance" (Acts 2:4). You will notice that it was "they" who did the speaking. The Holy Spirit did not do the speaking, the believers did. When you speak in tongues, you have to activate your voice. That will require moving your lips and your tongue, and beginning to speak. The Holy Spirit will empower you because the gift is in you waiting to get released, but you have to do the speaking. You will also notice in this verse that they *all* spoke in tongues. That means you can too. You are not being left out by God. Activate your faith and speak in tongues.

When I was released in the gift of tongues, I was by myself reading a book on the subject. I stepped out in faith at the end of reading the last chapter, and to my disappointment, only three syllables dribbled out through my lips. I questioned if I had truly received the gift, thinking maybe I had made up the sounds. I prayed again and still could only get those three syllables out. I repeated this a third time. Then I thought, *I only want to please God, and the Bible says that with faith I can please Him* (see Hebrews 11:6), *so I am going to believe these sounds are my tongues and I will be faithful with them.* The Word says that if you are faithful with a little, He will give you much (see Matthew 25:21). Every day I faithfully repeated the three syllables over and over, believing in my heart they were from God. Of course, the devil came with his lies, taunting me with thoughts like, *You sound ridiculous! You are just making this up!* The Holy Spirit helped me remain in faith so that every time a thought would come to my mind like that, I would pray with my three syllables even more. One day as I was driving down the street praying in my three syllables, a flood of language came forth, and I have been fully released ever since. God rewards faithfulness!

Believe me, praying in tongues will enhance your spiritual sensitivity and experience.

The Word of God

To be spiritual, we must have as much love and commitment to the Word of God (the Bible) as we do to Jesus Himself—who is Himself called "the Word" (see John 1:1–3). Jesus declared that the words He spoke were spirit and life (see John 6:63). We read that the universe was spoken into existence by the Word (see Hebrews 11:3; Genesis 1:3). The Word is spiritual, but its riches are manifested in natural ways.

In Luke 1:26–38 we are given a glimpse into the heavenly visitation Mary had when the angel Gabriel prophesied to her about her being chosen to give birth to Jesus. Mary had some questions, but concluded by declaring that nothing is impossible with God. She said, "May it be done to me according to your word" (verse 38). I love the way the Amplified Bible, Classic Edition expresses verse 37: "For with God nothing is ever impossible and no word from God shall be without power or impossible of fulfillment."

Further insight into the power of God's Word is found in Hebrews 4:12, here also in the Amplified Classic version:

> For the Word that God speaks is alive and full of power [making it active, operative, energizing, and effective]; it is sharper than any two-edged sword, penetrating to the dividing line of the breath of life (soul) and [the immortal] spirit, and of joints and marrow [of the deepest parts of our nature], exposing and sifting and analyzing and judging the very thoughts and purposes of the heart.
>
> Hebrews 4:12 AMPC

Reading the Word, studying the Word, meditating on the Word, and activating the Word will spiritualize you because God's Word is spirit. Spend time each day getting filled with the Word.

Benefits of Being Filled with the Word

1. You will be filled with the life of Christ (see John 6:63).
2. You will experience divine creativity (see Genesis 1:1–3).
3. You will be stable (see Psalm 1:2).
4. You will yield fruit (see Psalm 1:3).
5. Your heart will always be fresh, never dry (see Psalm 1:3).

6. You will experience supernatural prosperity (see Psalm 1:3).
7. You will have a clear path to walk on in life (see Psalm 119:105).
8. You will be revived (see Psalm 119:107).
9. You will be sustained with God's life (see Psalm 119:116).
10. You will be filled with light (see Psalm 119:130).

A Spiritual Person Loves Both the Word and the Spirit

When I teach people how to engage in heavenly encounter, I always emphasize the importance of focusing on both the Word and the Spirit. The Word of God will reveal the realities of the heavenly dimension. The Spirit of God will guide you into heavenly encounters and will open your eyes to behold the glories that await you. By loving both Word and Spirit, you accelerate your spiritual growth and you will have ease engaging in heavenly encounters.

The fact is that when you were born again, you ceased being an earthly being attempting to get into heaven—you became a heavenly being living on the earth. You are now a supernatural being. You are spiritual. Accessing heavenly riches comes through spiritual activation. The natural flesh cannot access the riches of Christ Jesus, but you can!

When you are established in Christ and are committed to living as a supernatural being, you can fill the earth with heavenly riches. In the next chapter, you will be commissioned to bless the earth with His glory.

SUMMARY

1. While on earth, Jesus preached the Kingdom of God, taught the Kingdom of God and demonstrated the Kingdom of God by the power of the Holy Spirit. He was deeply spiritual, committed to only doing on the earth the things He saw His Father do in heaven.
2. He said that we, His disciples, would do even greater things, yet we will only be able to do them if we, like He, are deeply spiritual.
3. True spiritual believers will regularly experience and minister healings, deliverances, prophetic words and dreams, speak in tongues and enjoy encounters in the glory realm. This is normal for the spiritual Christian.
4. To be spiritual, we must be filled and empowered by the Spirit. If we are going to receive from God and enjoy continual access to His heavenly riches, we must invite the Holy Spirit to have first place in our lives.
5. Benefits of being filled with the Spirit include *dynamis* power to activate miracles, boldness to preach, access to the open heaven, guidance, revelation of eternal truth and much more.
6. An evidence of being baptized in the Holy Spirit is the gift of tongues. It is received and released by faith. Praying in tongues has many benefits; when you pray in tongues you are personally spiritually empowered and edified, you come to understand divine mysteries and you pray perfect prayers that are according to the agenda of heaven.
7. To be spiritual, one must have a love and commitment to the Word of God. The Word is spiritual and life-giving.

Reading the Word, studying the Word, meditating on the Word and activating the Word will spiritualize you because God's Word is spirit.

QUESTIONS TO PONDER

1. In light of this chapter, do you consider yourself to be "religious" or truly spiritual? Explain your answer.
2. If you have been baptized in the Holy Spirit, how has it changed your life and how you touch the lives of others? Do you pray in tongues? If not, has this chapter helped you to have a clearer picture and faith for it?
3. What is your relationship with the Word? Do you love it and are you committed to it? Re-read the benefits listed above and reflect on how each of these are reflected in your own life.

MAKE THIS DECLARATION OVER YOUR LIFE

I am a spiritual, supernatural, heavenly being living on earth. Like Jesus while here on earth, I am empowered by the Holy Spirit. According to His promise, by His Spirit I have the power to do even greater things than He did. I am anointed to preach and give witness with boldness and with demonstrations of power. Because I love both the Word and the Spirit, I will accelerate in spiritual growth and will have ease engaging in heavenly encounters.

10

Filling the Earth with the Riches of Heaven

> For the earth will be filled with the knowledge of the glory of the LORD, as the waters cover the sea.
>
> Habakkuk 2:14

I was with a street team in Phoenix, Arizona, sharing the Gospel. A school bus stopped and let off several young people in their mid-teens who sat down on the bus bench to wait for another bus. Once they were parked on the bench, we greeted them with the love of God. One of the team members, who had earlier received a prophetic word of knowledge[1] for a specific young man, pointed at him and said, "You had a sports injury that hurt your back." The boy was shocked to the core. He shouted, "How did you know?" The team member explained that it was Jesus who had revealed it to him and that Jesus could heal him. Jesus did indeed heal him, right there at the bus stop. His friends gathered around and we ended up having revival on the street as healing and words of prophetic destiny were released and God brought salvation to the teens. What heavenly riches were poured out that day!

Believers are anointed and appointed by God to bring good news to the afflicted—to bless the earth with the true riches of heaven.

> The Spirit of the Lord God is upon me, because the Lord has anointed me to bring good news to the afflicted; He has sent me to bind up the brokenhearted, to proclaim liberty to captives and freedom to prisoners; to proclaim the favorable year of the Lord and the day of vengeance of our God; to comfort all who mourn, to grant those who mourn in Zion, giving them a garland instead of ashes, the oil of gladness instead of mourning, the mantle of praise instead of a spirit of fainting. So they will be called oaks of righteousness, the planting of the Lord, that He may be glorified.
>
> Isaiah 61:1–3

God wants every part of the earth to be filled with the knowledge of His glory, but He has not appointed angels, heavenly creatures or the elders in heaven to release the riches of His Gospel to those who do not know Him—He unlocks the riches of heaven through His Church! Angels can help us and heaven can cheer us on, but heavenly beings are not the ones who are commissioned to proclaim the Gospel of His Kingdom and glory to the earth. We are!

Light Belongs in the Darkness

Isaiah prophesied that those who had received the light (Jesus) would arise and shine and invade the dark earth and its people with His glory (see Isaiah 60:1–3). God wants the entire world to come to Him. Every knee will bow and every tongue will confess that Jesus is Lord (see Philippians 2:10–11).

Many born-again believers love spending time in church activities and being engaged in fellowship with believers. These things are wonderful, but we should not get so comfortable in church life that we fail to bring His light to those who will never know Him unless we go to them.

Jesus never said, "Stay ye in all the church," but rather, "Go ye into all the world" (Mark 16:15 KJV). Let's access the riches of heaven and then go out and bless the world with the fullness of all that He is and all that He has. Whether we reach out in big or small ways, we can obey Jesus every day of our lives.

A number of years ago, we hosted an outreach in the inner city of Vancouver, Canada. It was a very dark and dangerous place, like many inner cities, plagued with gross corruption, murder, addiction, prostitution, sex trafficking and more. The week before the start of the evangelism school and outreach, we first walked the streets and prayed. You could feel the tangible weight of the effects of sin in the region and it was hard to observe so many people who were bound and tormented in this demonic atmosphere. The devil's realm is full of darkness; he is a cruel taskmaster who keeps people from seeing the light and glory of God's Kingdom.

We rented a room in a slum hotel right in the heart of the corruption. One of the women with me resisted the idea.

She said, "Just down the street is a high-end section of the city; Let's stay there."

I responded, "I totally understand your apprehension, but what did Jesus do when He came from heaven to earth to reach us? Our light belongs right in the middle of the darkness. That is the best way to invade it with His love."

Jesus is our model for "incarnational evangelism." He did not remain in heaven and just pour down some blessings upon us. He left all the comforts of heavenly glory and came to the earth "as us," yet without sin. Everyone on the streets could tell that we were "straight"—we had to earn their trust by identifying with them, like Jesus, without sinning.

We walked the streets hour after hour, inviting God to share His heart with us concerning those we saw there. At first the people who lived in the area did not trust us, but after the first couple of days, they could feel our love and many testified that we were "safe." We took a number of them out for coffee and meals one-on-one and invited them to share their hearts, their pain and their shattered dreams. One by one, we saw God invade the hopelessness.

After the first few days, the atmosphere of the region shifted in some ways. Although the darkness was still present, the glory of God was becoming more prevalent and individuals were being transformed. Joy was filling the streets. Heavenly riches of peace, healing and deliverance were permeating the atmosphere. As individuals received miracles, destiny words and spiritual encouragement, the Gospel was evident on practically every street corner, in the back allies, slum hotel lobbies and restaurants. Many gave their hearts to Jesus. The light of heaven invaded the darkness.

We were working with a local ministry that had relentlessly preached the Gospel, fed and clothed the poor and served as a true light in the area for many years. Many came to them for help. They had interceded faithfully and preached the Gospel to those who were destitute. They had paved the way in the Spirit for this wonderful week of outreach and they were able to follow up afterward. Our presence, partnership and service were refreshing for them. The unity of believers helped bring the riches of heaven into the darkness of earth (see Psalm 133:1[2]).

Light Invades a Porn Convention

A friend of mine is very passionate about taking the love of Jesus to those who are bound by darkness. I partnered with her on an outreach at a pornography convention in Las Vegas, Nevada. The convention hosted 25,000 registrants from around the world, including porn stars, producers, directors, distributors, merchants and consumers. We rented a booth for the five-day convention right in the middle of the central vendors hall. We were not there to promote or imbibe the darkness of the porn industry and neither were we there to preach hellfire and damnation—we were there to be a light in the midst of darkness and to demonstrate the love of God.

We set up a booth to offer participants "destiny words" and dream interpretation. In many Spirit-filled churches, believers receive prophetic words revealing God's plan and purpose for them, but most people outside the Church have never received a word from God. God wants to speak to everyone, no matter how deeply they are steeped in darkness;

in fact, one word from God's heart can deliver a person into a brand-new life in Christ. God's love is the greatest treasure in heaven, and He wants us to access the riches of His love for those who are trapped in sin and bondage: "For God so loved the world, that He gave His only begotten Son, that whoever believes in Him shall not perish, but have eternal life" (John 3:16).

Streams of people came to our booth to "hear from God," and as we revealed His heart, their hearts were tenderized and a number of them wept. Many who had once walked with God but had turned away from Him returned.

At the end of the event, my friend was packing up some of the last supplies when the coordinator of the event approached her. He said, "We have been hearing some great reports about your booth—you have made a great impact. We would like to invite you to come to a convention in another city where there will be over 75,000 participants." They conversed and she was able to share God's love with him personally. He was deeply touched. Although he did not receive the Lord at that moment, the eternal seed was planted. He experienced the presence of God. Because of her faithfulness, he was able to receive a taste of God's riches—the greatest of all His riches—*love*.

Psychic Fairs

Why do people go to psychics? Before I was born again, I went to a number of them because I was hungry to know what my future had in store for me. People do not go to psychics because they want to find out about all the bad things life might offer; rather, they go expecting to hear good things.

Why? Because innately they know that God is good and He has good things for their lives, they just do not yet know who God is.

That is why we need to go to the dark places to bring truth into the midst of error. People who attend psychic fairs are looking for supernatural encounter, so we need to be there to reveal heavenly riches and the truth of Christ.

When we started engaging in prophetic evangelism back in the 1990s, psychic fairs were a favorite outreach. Prophetic teams would rent booths and offer "Free Spiritual Readings." The lines at the Christian booths were always longer than the others, and God always touched lives and amazed people. Once someone is in awe of what has just been revealed, it is easy to lead them to Jesus.

One time a seasoned psychic came to my table. He said, "You have great light around you—such light I have never seen. You have a very high-level spirit guide." I responded, "Yes, I have the highest-level spirit guide in the universe and I can introduce you to Him." You might be shocked at my response, but it is the truth: The Holy Spirit *is* our guide. The Scripture says that He will lead and *guide* us into all truth (see John 16:13[3]). When Jesus walked the earth, He spoke to people in ways they could relate to. He spoke to farmers about wheat and fishermen about fish. I was not coming into this psychic's realm of darkness; I was inviting him into the light to experience true riches.

I gave him a prophetic word sourced in Jesus and he was blown away. He was shocked by the "energy" he felt from me. He then told me a dream that he had never been able to understand. The Lord gave me an interpretation for him and again he was in awe. Eventually, after sharing for a while, the revelation of Christ came to both him and his wife, and they gave their hearts to Jesus. He was looking for Jesus all along—he just never knew it. I also shared with him about the Holy Spirit and he became hungry for the Holy Spirit as well. He and his wife had encountered the riches of heaven, and they not only received Christ but wanted to know more about the Holy Spirit and His gifts.

This man was created by God to be a prophet, but the enemy had tried to use him for his own purposes. Most psychics were created to be prophets, but they have been deceived. Let's go find them and reveal the truth!

Human Trafficking

We read in Revelation 18 the Lord's disclosure about the last days. He reveals the corruption of the world system and announces that it will be destroyed by fire in one day (see verses 8–10). He also lists the commodities of the earthly merchants, and one of them is "the trafficking of the bodies and souls of people":

> The earth's merchants weep and mourn for her because no one buys their merchandise anymore: their gold, silver, jewels, and pearls, their fine linen, purple cloth, silk, and scarlet cloth, all kinds of things made from expensive wood, ivory, bronze, iron, and marble, quantities of the finest cinnamon, spice, incense, frankincense, and myrrh, wine, olive oil, wheat, and the finest flour, sheep, cattle, horses, and their four-wheeled carriages, *and the trafficking of the bodies and souls of people.*
>
> Revelation 18:11–13 TPT, emphasis added

When we first started to work in the field of human trafficking, it was very difficult to convince most people that it was actually happening. But before long, the media began to report and confirm the truth about the industry.

Human trafficking targets people, both male and female, of all ages. We have seen frail, elderly and malnourished people trafficked to be beggars on the streets, only to give all they collect to their handlers. We have seen women, babies, young men, young women and children of all ages being trafficked. All of it is heart-wrenching; but when we discovered how children were being so cruelly exploited, that is what motivated us to become a voice for them.

Our first encounter with the trafficking of children for sex, labor and organs was in Thailand and Cambodia. Although human trafficking is a worldwide industry that involves almost every nation in some way, we discovered that there are epicenters for the trade. Thailand was a major distributor of sex-trafficked victims at the time, and Cambodia was a targeted location to find the victims.

Traffickers would go into poor villages and slums and lie to the parents of the children. As I shared in a previous chapter, they might say something like, "You have so many children to feed and you are so poor. Let me pay you $10 for one of your children so you can buy rice for the others and I will take your child to a rich family in Thailand who will raise and educate them. When they are older, they will come back and care for you and the family." Back in the day, very few of the families understood what was really happening. The trafficker would drug that child and others and smuggle them across the border often in the bottom of wooden carts with heaps of blankets piled on top. When they got through to the other side, they would then distribute the children to handlers for slave labor, illegal organ donations or private adoptions, or to brothels for purposes of prostitution, creation of porn productions or even to global sex auctions.

One of our first assignments was to make the parents aware. We would go into the villages and share what was really happening. We educated them on what to do if they were approached. Many do not sell their children now, but unfortunately, others still do; some even discovered that if they resisted at first, they could get more money from the traffickers. It could increase to $30 per child, then $100 then $300, eventually in some cases $1000 or more. Some women even would get pregnant deliberately in order to sell a child to the trafficker. This is gross darkness.

One child we had the opportunity to help usher into freedom was sold by his own mother at two years of age. I will call him Tony. We found him when he was approximately ten years old. Medical examiners confirmed that he had been a victim of forced labor and had also been used for sex. He was drugged regularly; with needle scars all over his body to confirm it. (Handlers will often use three types of drugs on boys: One is a stimulant to keep them awake and hyperactive so they can work longer and harder; another is a sedative when they are transporting them so they will not try to run away, and the third is a drug to sexually stimulate the little boys because they are too young to sexually perform for the handler's clients.) It was believed that our little Tony was used for forced labor during the day and then was required to serve sexual clients at night.

He was traumatized and demonized in many ways, body, soul and spirit. He had never known love, but he was a survivor. After he was rescued, God's love transformed him and miracles of healing and deliverance unfolded. He had never been educated, but he excelled in the homeschooling program we gave him; in fact, his marks were higher than the national standard for his age. Love transformed him and discipled him. He experienced the riches of heaven! Today he is a wonderful young man. He still has some difficulties to overcome, but he wears a beautiful smile and is safe. Tony's life and story have touched many.

Every child is one of God's treasures. When we look at a child through God's eyes, we will see their potential and be able to breathe life into them. Moses was a child at risk, but the midwives and his mother and sister fought for him, and Pharaoh's daughter took him in. The Scripture says that his parents saw that he was a beautiful child: "By faith Moses, when he was born, was hidden three months by his parents, because they saw he was a beautiful child; and they were not afraid of the king's command" (Hebrews 11:23 NKJV). They saw that he was a treasure, and generations are so glad they did.

We have seen child after child rescued from the most horrific and evil situations. Each one of them is God's treasure—each one of them carries valuable destiny and potential. The Church is being compelled by the Spirit to reach them. If we search for them, we will find them—God will make sure of it! Some of the rescues we have seen have been so supernatural that there is no way in the natural that the children would be found apart from God's intervention.

Today, God's glory is being poured out in the earth into some of the darkest places. He has given us access to everything that we need to bring His light, healing, deliverance and life to the earth.

Let's Invade the Darkness

Look around you. There is darkness everywhere, but you are a person who can change it, because you have access to God's riches in heaven. You can help fill the earth with the knowledge of the glory of the Lord. The only reason why there is still darkness on the earth is simply because it has not yet been invaded with His light.

Let's invade the darkness. Let's utilize every promise that is available to us and fill the earth with His brilliance. You might not be able to go find trafficked victims and you might not be called to porn festivals, psychic fairs, or inner cities, but you are called somewhere. There is light in you. You have access to the riches of heaven. Find some darkness in your sphere of influence and invade it with light! You are a carrier of His glory, a carrier of His riches. *Go*! Let heaven's resources fill the earth through *you*!

> Then the seventh angel sounded: And there were loud voices in heaven, saying, "The kingdoms of this world have become the kingdoms of our Lord and of His Christ, and He shall reign forever and ever!"
>
> Revelation 11:15 NKJV

SUMMARY

1. Believers are anointed and appointed by God to bring good news to the afflicted—to bless the earth with heaven's true riches. God wants every part of the earth to be filled with the knowledge of His glory, and He unlocks the riches of heaven through His Church!

2. We must not get so comfortable in church programs and activities that we fail to bring His light to those who will never know Him or His riches unless we go out to them.
3. There are countless opportunities to bring the light into the darkness. We can go to slums, conventions or fairs that celebrate evil or perversion; places where human trafficking is practiced—or to our own neighborhoods and families.
4. God has given us access to everything that we need to bring His light, healing, deliverance and life into the earth.
5. As one who is called to be a carrier of God's glory and riches, find some darkness in your sphere of influence. Invade it with light! Let the riches of heaven fill the earth through *you*.

QUESTIONS TO PONDER

1. Did you and/or loved ones encounter God's light and riches because someone reached out to you? How has your (their) life changed because of this?
2. Is there an area of need and darkness where you feel particularly drawn to take God's light and His riches? What draws you there? Have you followed through yet? If not, what is hindering you and how do you plan to overcome it?
3. Do you still have fear, or feel powerless to invade the darkness with God's light? If, so, review these chapters

and take inventory of everything you have access to as a child of God. What steps do you need to take to make them an inner reality?

MAKE THIS DECLARATION OVER YOUR LIFE

As a child of God, I am a supernaturally empowered heavenly being with access to all of the riches of Heaven—God's promises, His provision, His blessings, His power. Heaven is open to me and I am a carrier of God's riches; the earth can be filled with those riches through me. I am a carrier of God's light and I invade the darkness of the world with His brilliance. I am a carrier of God's glory, and I know that the earth will be filled with the knowledge of His glory.

Notes

Chapter 1: On Earth as It Is in Heaven

1. "Although He existed in the form of God, [Jesus] did not regard equality with God a thing to be grasped, but emptied Himself, taking the form of a bond-servant, and being made in the likeness of men. Being found in appearance as a man, He humbled Himself by becoming obedient to the point of death, even death on a cross" (Philippians 2:6–8).

2. "The Son of God appeared for this purpose, to destroy the works of the devil" (1 John 3:8).

3. Bill Johnson, *The Way of Life: Experiencing the Culture of Heaven on Earth* (Shippensburg: Destiny Image, 2018), 7.

4. "Truly, truly, I say to you, he who believes in Me, the works that I do, he will do also; and greater works than these he will do; because I go to the Father" (John 14:12).

Chapter 2: Hindrances to Accessing the Riches of Heaven

1. A portal is an opening, like a door or window. Jacob in Genesis 28 saw a portal opened into heaven and a ladder extending from earth into heaven.

2. Spiritual gift that enables believers to speak in a heavenly language. See 1 Corinthians 12:4–7; 1 Corinthians 14:2–4; Mark 16:15–17.

3. "Whatever is not from faith is sin" (Romans 14:23).

Chapter 3: Heaven's Abundant Life

1. "Jesus said to him, 'I am the way, and the truth, and the life; no one comes to the Father but through Me'" (John 14:6).

Chapter 4: Four Realms of Abundance

1. A *tithe* is 10 percent. The tithe given to God is the first 10 percent of a believer's increase.

Chapter 5: Creating Realms of Abundance

1. See also 1 Peter 5:6–10.

2. "This is the confidence which we have before Him, that, if we ask anything according to His will, He hears us. And if we know that He hears us in whatever we ask, we know that we have the requests which we have asked from Him" (1 John 5:14–15).

3. "For as the rain and the snow come down from heaven, and do not return there without watering the earth and making it bear and sprout, and furnishing seed to the sower and bread to the eater; so will My word be which goes forth from My mouth; it will not return to Me empty, without accomplishing what I desire, and without succeeding in the matter for which I sent it" (Isaiah 55:10–11).

Chapter 6: Accessing the Riches of Heaven by Faith

1. As translated from the Aramaic. It is possible to translate the Greek text as an adjectival phrase, "God-like faith" or "godly faith." (Footnote on Mark 11:22, Brian Simmons, *The Passion Translation*, BroadStreet, 2017.)

2. "O my dove, in the clefts of the rock, in *the secret place* of the steep pathway, let me see your form, let me hear your voice; for your voice is sweet, and your form is lovely" (Song of Solomon 2:14, emphasis added).

Chapter 7: Ascending and Descending

1. "Or do you not know that your body is a temple of the Holy Spirit who is in you, whom you have from God, and that you are not your own?" (1 Corinthians 6:19).

2. God's instruction for building the tabernacle is found in Exodus chapters 25, 26 and 27.

3. "And behold, the veil of the temple was torn in two from top to bottom; and the earth shook and the rocks were split" (Matthew 27:51).

Chapter 8: Accessing Riches in Heaven through Praise and Worship

1. Ruth Ward Heflin, *Glory—Experiencing the Atmosphere of Heaven*, Kindle location 102,104.

2. Strong's Online Concordance, "tehillah," H8416.

3. Strong's Online Concordance, "aineō," G134.

4. Strong's Online Concordance, "hymneo," G5214.

5. Jesus said, "But an hour is coming, and now is, when the true worshipers will worship the Father in spirit and truth; for such people the Father seeks to be His worshipers. God is spirit, and those who worship Him must worship in spirit and truth" (John 4:23–24).

Chapter 9: Be Spiritual

1. "After being baptized, Jesus came up immediately from the water; and behold, the heavens were opened, and he saw the Spirit of God descending as a dove and lighting on Him" (Matthew 3:16).

2. Strong's Online Concordance, "*dynamis*," G1411.
3. Strong's Online Concordance, "*baptizo*," G907.

Chapter 10: Filling the Earth with the Riches of Heaven

1. The word of knowledge is one of the gifts of the Holy Spirit listed in 1 Corinthians 12:7–10.

2. "Behold, how good and how pleasant it is for brothers to dwell together in unity!" (Psalm 133:1).

3. "When He, the Spirit of truth, comes, He will *guide* you into all the truth; for He will not speak on His own initiative, but whatever He hears, He will speak; and He will disclose to you what is to come" (John 16:13, emphasis added).

Patricia King is a respected apostolic and prophetic minister of the Gospel, a successful business owner and an inventive entrepreneur. She is an accomplished itinerant speaker, author, television host, media producer and ministry network overseer who has given her life fully to Jesus Christ and to the advancement of His Kingdom on the earth. She is the founder of Patricia King Ministries and co-founder of XPmedia.com.

Website

www.patriciaking.com

Email:

email: Info@patriciaking.com

Facebook

www.facebook.com/patriciakingpage

Twitter

@patriciaking4JC